D0199870

Bettie Bradley

Editor, *Today's Bride*

The Wedding Expert

400 Things

You Need to Know

to Plan Your

Big Day

appetite

by RANDOM HOUSE

COPYRIGHT © 2014 BETTIE BRADLEY

All rights reserved. The use of any part of this publication, reproduced, transmitted
in any form or by any means electronic, mechanical, photocopying, recording or otherwise,
or stored in a retrieval system without the prior written consent of the publisher—or in
the case of photocopying or other reprographic copying, license from the Canadian
Copyright Licensing Agency—is an infringement of the copyright law.

Appetite by Random House® is a registered trademark
of Random House LLC.

Library and Archives of Canada Cataloguing in Publication is available upon request.

Print ISBN: 978-0-449-01638-1
e-book ISBN: 978-0-449-01639-8

Original fashion illustrations © 2014 Danielle Meder

Printed and bound in the USA

Published in Canada by Appetite by Random House®,
A division of Random House of Canada Limited,
A Penguin Random House Company
www.penguinrandomhouse.ca

appetite   Penguin
by RANDOM HOUSE   Random
House

10 9 8 7 6 5 4 3 2 1

To my children: John, Jane and Meghan.
They are my cheerleaders, as I am theirs.

Contents

Thirty-five years ago . . . the bride still lived with her parents, was young, inexperienced and often accustomed to saying, "Yes, Mother."

Weddings Then, Weddings Now

Thirty-five Years of Change

Thirty-five years ago, when I covered a wedding for *Today's Bride* magazine, it was easy: I just had a chat with the mother-of-the-bride. She was in control. And why not? Usually, the bride still lived with her parents and was young, inexperienced and accustomed to saying, "Yes, Mother." And anyway—Dad was paying all the bills.

The joke, at the time, was that the groom's role was to buy or rent a suit and show up. And what about the groom's family? I remember a friend of mine calling and saying, "My son's getting married. What's the role of the mother-of-the-groom?" My reply? Call the bride's mother and ask her what color dress she will be wearing, because she has first choice. So there, in a nutshell, was pretty much what was expected of the groom *and* his family all those years ago: show up and shut up.

(In fairness, there were two relatively minor expectations. The groom's parents were expected to host an intimate dinner to meet the bride's parents, and an informal dinner after the wedding rehearsal.)

The gift registry was pretty new on the scene, and guess who made the choices? The mothers' influence was so strong that major china manufacturers, such as Royal Doulton, Wedgwood and Noritake, produced special patterns that were marketed as "bridal collections." These were designed to appeal to the mothers' generation and were inevitably pretty floral patterns in pastel colors.

The bridal couple likely met through friends or their church or had been school sweethearts. If they didn't share the same religion, people whispered and wondered how long the marriage could last. If they didn't have the same ethnic background, that was also ominous: "What a shame! The parents must be so disappointed!" And as for same-sex marriage . . . you're kidding, right?

Now fast-forward three-and-a-half decades. The bride is older—edging up to age thirty—and almost certainly doesn't live with her parents. In fact, many couples are already living together. These older couples choose to be established in their careers before getting married. And more than 50 percent of all of today's bridal couples pay for, and therefore host, their own wedding.

Check out the variables of today's weddings. There may be no specific religious affiliation and the couple has a civil service or hires freelance clergy to perform the service. Sometimes couples don't share the same faith and so they either negotiate which one will prevail or ensure both religions are represented at the service. And if they have different ethnic backgrounds, they accommodate the expectations of both. And then look at the brief history of same-sex marriage, which is now legally accepted in many countries around the world.

The influence of electronic communication, including social media, is also changing or modifying how today's weddings are planned. While in most cases the proposal news will be shared with parents first—and best of all, in person—you likely will rely on your smartphone to share the news with friends. But, remember that wedding invitations must be sent by mail. Shower and other party invitations may be sent electronically, but when it comes to the big day, do it the right way—with real paper, envelopes and postage!

There are many smartphone apps and websites to help you plan your wedding. Some allow you to collect images and get planning ideas. One acts like your own personal social media hub, where your guests can meet and share stories while you keep them updated. Another may make gift-giving for your guests easy, allowing you the flexibility of adding items from more than one store by using your phone as a barcode scanner and choosing items from anywhere in the world.

The vast variety of today's weddings raises a practical question: "Does etiquette matter? Is there any place for the traditional rules of wedding behavior today?" The truthful answer is no. The set-in-stone rules of etiquette do not matter. They have been replaced with guidelines.

These guidelines are meant to make everyone involved in the wedding feel wanted and comfortable. They are meant to help make the day seamless. They are a practical way to avoid disappointment while you invent your own wedding.

So, the world turns! In my years in the world of bridal I have seen and watched and even sometimes influenced the changes when I saw a trend that I thought needed a little support. This book is my gift to couples that could use a little hand-holding as they plan their big day. I hope you will find the answers to your questions as you turn the pages of *The Wedding Expert: 400 Things You Need to Know to Plan Your Big Day*.

Your engagement is a life-changing event because it affects all your relationships, especially those that matter most to you.

One

The Engagement

It's just the beginning

t begins the moment the ring is slipped on your finger. The proposal may be expected—there's a possibility that you looked at rings together and perhaps you hinted at what you wanted. Or maybe the proposal is a true surprise. Regardless, you are likely experiencing a mix of feelings—anywhere from relief and "Finally!" to panic and an unexpected worry: "Is this really the person I want to spend the rest of my life with?"

The initial reaction is followed by excitement and a call to action: "I must tell everyone!" You want everybody to know, from your parents to your best friends to the people at work (and especially that one woman at the office who didn't think you'd ever get him to the altar). You suddenly want to text *everyone*, but who you tell first is important.

Share the news of your engagement first with those most important to you. It's important that your parents hear the words "We wanted you to be the first to know," and that your fiancé's mom and dad are second on your list. After that, it follows in order of who is most important in your life. Maybe it's a grandmother, a sister or brother or your best friend, but remember that the order in which you announce your engagement to friends and family matters to them—and it will be remembered.

BETTIEQUETTE:

Avoid announcing your engagement on social media until you've shared the news with your parents.

Know that things are going to change. There will be subtle changes in your relationships with almost everybody. This may come as a huge surprise to you. Be aware that when someone hears life-changing news from a person who matters to them, their first thought, even subconsciously, may be, "How does this affect me?" It's just human nature. So don't be surprised if some of your friends feel that they are losing a little of you.

Be sensitive to the feelings of your close friends. Your friends will *ooh* and *aah* over the ring, but a nagging thought may be at the back of their minds: "Everything between us is going to change."

Be considerate of this feeling. You're enjoying being the center of attention, but it's not all about you. Your engagement and imminent wedding and marriage will affect your relationships with others, and from their point of view, not always in a positive way.

Understand that there will be a subtle change in your relationship with your parents. If you are planning to marry the person your parents would have chosen for you, you will suddenly be grown-up in their eyes as they welcome you to the club. If your parents feel you have chosen the wrong person, however, get ready for a reserved reaction. If they have given up trying to influence you, they will struggle with acceptance. Be patient. Plan events that will bring you all together so they may finally understand your choice of life partner.

Tread carefully with your future mother-in-law. Every mother of a son has a mental picture of the type of woman her son deserves— and in fact, the type of daughter-in-law that *she* deserves! You may come close to that image, or you may not. Either way, your relationship with your fiancé's mother in the coming months will set the pattern for the years ahead. If she is intrusive, how will you handle this? If she is distant, how can you get her to warm up so a closer relationship can be established?

Watch for signals that the relationship may be drifting to a place that will cause challenges throughout your married life. Take the lead in setting up the relationship you want to have in the long term. Have one-on-one lunches with her. Take her into your confidence with the wedding plans. Listen to her advice. Why not? You don't have to act on it!

Host a dinner to bring the bride's and groom's parents together. This is the time to share some of your wedding plans. Traditionally, the groom's parents hosted this dinner, but if you, as the bridal couple, are planning and underwriting the costs of your own wedding, don't stand on ceremony.

BETTIEQUETTE:
It doesn't matter who hosts a dinner to introduce both sets of parents—just make sure that this dinner takes place.

Surprise! Your relationship with your fiancé will change. Until you decided to marry, you had the fun and excitement of getting to know each other, meeting each other's friends and family, sharing thoughts and dreams, perhaps playing house together.

Now you're making a commitment that is meant to be forever. This is serious stuff and you may each react in a different, and

About 30 percent of engaged couples today will already have bought, or are about to buy, a house.

surprising, way. One of you could have second thoughts from time to time. It may be the bride, it may be the groom, but it's almost inevitable. Don't panic. Even if you have been living together, this legal step is huge and can feel overwhelming. Hang in there, confide in a best friend—and if the relationship is right, these doubts will pass.

Avoid making immediate decisions about who will be in the wedding party. Too many friendships go off the rails because of premature and impulsive invitations extended to the wrong people and later retracted.

It's not unusual for couples who have been married ten years to have lost touch with their wedding attendants and, in some cases, to have trouble remembering their names! They made the mistake of impulsively inviting new and exciting friends or co-workers to be in the wedding party and overlooked siblings and longtime friends.

Be aware of taking advantage of co-workers during the months of planning. They will be happy for you and enjoy hearing the details. After all, they aren't as affected by your engagement as friends and family are, so for them it's a pleasant diversion to join in your excitement.

But what if your involvement in the minutiae of wedding planning results in some of your work ending up on their desks? What if they have to cover for you during those extra-long lunch hours when you're shopping for wedding accessories? There may be resentment. So be considerate. Your wedding planning should not come at your co-workers' expense.

Your boss may not be as thrilled as he or she appears to be. This can be a testing time. Some employers watch carefully to see how much emphasis a worker puts on wedding planning during business hours. How many phone calls? How much time spent online looking at wedding websites? How much wedding discussion with other staff members in the lunchroom? How many long lunch hours?

Take care. Your employer's assessment may be that you are putting your career on the back burner, and if so, you may be surprised to find yourself passed over for career opportunities, such as a hoped-for promotion.

Unwittingly, you may send a message that your job is just a way to make a living. And perhaps your intention really is to let your personal life take precedence. But if you have career ambitions, keep the wedding planning during work hours to a minimum and stay tuned in to your job.

BETTIEQUETTE:
Be certain that your boss doesn't hear about your engagement from other employees. Sit on your big news until you have a chance to tell him or her. Then share it with your co-workers.

Engagement Roundup

Consider how your engagement affects those around you.

~

Announce your engagement with joy, but also with sensitivity.

~

Don't assume that everyone will be overjoyed by the news.

~

Be prepared to have occasional misgivings.

~

Put a hold on choosing your attendants.

~

Fly under the radar at your workplace.

Without a budget, you're in big trouble, and that's a promise. Begin your wedding planning by allocating costs so there are no misunderstandings.

Two

The Budget

Establish who pays for what

There are a variety of options for financing today's weddings. Sometimes the cost is shared between the two sets of parents. Sometimes the cost is shared three ways, with each of the parents paying one third and the bridal couple paying one third. Sometimes the cost is entirely covered by the bridal couple.

Be aware that traditions are changing. Changes in the financing of weddings have introduced new and innovative ways for everyone to get their share of the spotlight. For example, if the bride and groom's parents jointly host the wedding, they are *both* hosts, and the groom's parents are no longer just guests and spectators. This should be reflected in the wording of the invitations and other courtesies shown to the groom's parents. Little by little, traditions are adjusting to the new reality of two families working in tandem with the bridal couple to produce the big event.

Sharing expenses. When the expenses are being shared, one of the most efficient approaches is for everyone to contribute equally to a wedding fund. Then, open one bank account from which all expenses will be paid.

The person handling the account must be totally accountable. Everything must be itemized once a month, and any unusual expense that does not appear on the approved budget should be discussed before the purchase.

Another way of sharing costs is for each contributor to choose the specific items for which they will be responsible. The groom's family may offer to pay for all the libations. The bride's parents may offer to pay for the food. The bridal couple may pay for the flowers and decor.

Develop a budget (see pages 21–24 for examples) and fill in estimated amounts for major items, then make a list of what still has to be covered.

Financing a wedding can cause major confrontations. The average wedding has 170 guests and the average cost is $25,000. Be clear from the start about the budget. Throughout the planning process, guidelines must be set up and adhered to. Be sensitive to the fact that family members may get more tense, irritable and even confrontational over money problems than over any other aspect of the planning.

Whoever pays the bills makes the monetary decisions. If either the bride's parents or both sets of parents decide to pay for the entire wedding, it then becomes a gift to the bridal couple—but one with potential strings attached. In such a case the bridal couple should refrain from exclaiming, "But it's our wedding!"

The couple can rule. More than half of today's weddings are financed by the bridal couple. This relates to the ages of the bride and groom. The average age has inched up to the late twenties. These older couples are no longer living in their parents' homes and are, increasingly, living together before marriage. They have definite ideas about the wedding and are prepared to host their own. This has resulted in a huge shift in who makes the decisions. In this instance, the couple rules. The parents are honored guests.

Who Decides What?
Let's be clear about who makes the decisions.

The size of the wedding. Whoever is paying the bills puts a cap on the size of the wedding. If the parents are paying and want a big bash, and the bridal couple wants a small intimate wedding, the bridal couple calls the shots. If the bridal couple wants a big wedding, the final decision rests with the person paying the bills.

The location of the ceremony. This decision is usually not a bone of contention, especially if the venue is a religious site. But sometimes the bridal couple chooses a secular site, such as an inn or hotel, a museum or art gallery, a private club or an outdoor venue like a park, and this is their decision—provided it does not involve extraordinary expense.

The reception site. The cost for the reception venue requires approval of the person signing the checks. The couple will undoubtedly have a preference, which should be considered and approved if the cost is not out of line. If the couple golfs, for instance, and wants the reception at their club, that is the appropriate choice if the price is right. If the venue is costly, however, the person funding the reception has a potential veto tucked in their back pocket!

The menu. The person picking up the tab for the big day decides how extensive the menu will be. (Is this becoming a tiresome song?) But the food preferences of the bride and groom should win the day, provided they are within the budget. However, if the groom wants to have Maine lobster flown in, and the person writing the check is happy with stuffed roast chicken, guess who wins?

The liquor and wine. A cash bar is unacceptable. It's an intolerably rude way to treat your guests. But the person who agrees to host the libations needs to have agreement on how much, where and when. If cost is a factor, have a tray service instead of an open bar during the cocktail reception and have only wine available during the dinner hour.

The color and theme of the wedding. This decision absolutely belongs to the bridal couple. This is not a monetary consideration, but one of personal taste and preference. The choice of color starts with the bridesmaids' gowns and extends to flowers and decor.

The flowers. This is a major cost, and the person picking up the tab should be on hand when the selections are made (although the bridal couple will choose the color theme before the visit to the florist).

The most significant cost will be for floral table centerpieces at the reception, although if there is a large wedding party, bouquets can be pricey, too. Many married couples in retrospect say that the flowers made their wedding day special, so budget a healthy amount.

How to Set a Budget

Step 1: Do your homework so you aren't just guesstimating. Clip out reception budgets that are available in most bridal magazines and online—or use the ones on pages 21–24. Eliminate items that don't apply to you, then add any extras that interest you. For example, most budgets will include a wedding cake and you may choose not to have one. On the other hand, it may not include table favors for guests, which may be important to you.

Step 2: Get on the phone with at least two companies in each category and have a chat about prices. National magazines can only give average prices across the country, so their estimates will not be specific to your area. Their suggested prices are a good starting point but you can narrow down the probable costs by doing your homework to create a good working budget.

Step 3: Set two budgets. Prepare one budget for the ceremony, bridal party and miscellaneous expenses. Prepare a separate budget for the reception.

The first budget will include your gown, veil, shoes and lingerie and your groom's attire. This budget should include any transportation costs (such as a limousine) and costs of the site, clergy, music and flowers. Don't forget to budget for gifts for your attendants and friends who are hosting showers for you.

The second budget is for the reception and will cover the food and bar, centerpieces, liquor license and the music or DJ.

Step 4: Hold a budget meeting. One of the current methods of sharing costs is to divide reception costs between the parents and have the bridal couple pay all the rest. Alternatively, all the expenses can be totaled and divided equally among the couple and their parents.

Parents don't need to be part of a budget meeting if they are not fiscally contributing, but if they are, set a meeting early in the planning process. If the bridal couple is paying for the entire wedding, only they need to have access to the budget. If parents are not contributing, it's frankly no concern of theirs how the money is spent.

How to Cut Costs

There are ways to keep a handle on costs that are so unnoticeable you will be glad you made the effort.

BETTIEQUETTE:

Wedding planners know the wedding market and which vendors give value. They also make great go-betweens when you're having family or vendor problems!

Be specific about your need for a professional wedding planner. The wedding planner has replaced the mother who once handled all the details. Today's mothers often have their own careers and their involvement is much less than it was just a generation ago.

Perhaps you have time to do it all yourself. And that could save you money. If you *don't* have time to do it all, trim costs by hiring a planner for specific parts of the process. You may not need one to coordinate everything from invitations to reception. Perhaps it's enough just to have a planner there on your wedding day to ensure that everything runs smoothly.

Limit the hours the bar is open. Having a cash bar is a faux pas, but there is no obligation for good hosts to offer an open bar from cocktail reception through dinner and throughout the after-dinner dance. Instead, have a tray service with cocktails at the cocktail party, have wine only during dinner, and then open the bar after the dinner and toasts are over.

BETTIEQUETTE:

Let me say this again: Having a cash bar is not an acceptable way to cut costs.

Monitor the bartender. See that the empty bottles are counted at the end of the reception. Not the next day—that same evening. It's wise to conduct the count alongside the bartender and have him or her sign off on the agreed total.

Having a second set of eyes—perhaps a member of the family—on alcohol consumption at the end of the night can save hundreds of dollars, because, sadly, some bartenders inflate the bottle count.

Trim the number of blooms. Flowers are a major expense, but costs can be controlled. It is the blooms that cost, not the fill (such as baby's breath). Cut down on the number of flowers in each bouquet or in your table centers. Ask the florist to show you examples of lovely bouquets and centerpieces that have fewer blooms. You may be pleasantly surprised.

Use flowers that are in season. Roses are popular. Quite apart from being the flower of love and staying fresh throughout a long day, they are readily available year-round. Flowers that have to come from the greenhouse or from abroad escalate the cost.

Think outside the flower centerpiece. Interesting centerpiece alternatives include two or three feeder fish swimming in rented fishbowls, or clustered pillar candles (if the site allows candles), or even crystal bowls heaped with tasty treats for your guests to enjoy.

Don't accept anything just because "it's tradition." Use only those services or traditions that are important to you and you'll see a measurable decrease in your budget.

Is a wedding cake a must-have for you? In my own family, both of my daughters said they didn't want a cake. They preferred an unusual dessert for their guests. They decided that its omission would not be noticed—and they were right. On the other hand, when my son was married, having a cake was number one on his and his bride's must-have list.

My daughters (determined and independent thinkers!) did not feel tied to tradition and carefully picked only what they felt put their stamp on their special day. One daughter invited close friends and family to contribute their best homemade treats for a midnight dessert buffet. A close friend of mine had a do-it-yourself ice cream sundae bar, which was a lot of fun!

Choose cars over limousines. My daughters felt that paying for limousines was a waste of money when their family and friends had perfectly fine cars. Not surprisingly, their brother and his fiancée loved the idea of limousines!

Limit the number of courses in the meal. People today don't have the large appetites of past generations. It is enough to offer, say, three courses of good quality. Nobody needs a five-course dinner. Have either a delicious soup or a creative salad, but you don't need both.

Cut a deal with your photographer. See if you can pay for photography services, buy the prints and prepare your own albums. This not only saves money but allows you to decide which photos you want to mount and frame to be displayed on your walls, and which you want tucked safely away in an album.

Trim music costs. Music is an essential element of most wedding services and receptions. You are wise to budget for music that will set the right mood for both events. You will pay extra if you want the church musician(s) at the rehearsal, but most professionals who regularly play for weddings don't feel their attendance at the rehearsal is necessary. Outline your specific choices at a meeting with the musicians.

For music at the reception, you may have a DJ or you may prefer a live band. If a band stretches your budget, give your local high school a ring. They could have a small, experienced band that is of excellent quality. Students love to pick up a little money and additional experience.

Some cities also have groups of talented amateurs who perform in parks in summer and also enjoy earning extra cash at weddings.

Choose any day but Saturday for your wedding. This may not be a concession you are willing to make, but ask almost any reception site about the discounts you get for a weekday or Sunday wedding. These are substantial!

Have a daytime wedding and reception. The time of day can make a huge difference to your budget. The most expensive weddings include a dinner and dance reception. If you wish to cut costs, consider a late-morning ceremony followed by a lunch or an early afternoon wedding followed by either afternoon tea or a cocktail party.

Order wine by the case or magnum. Instead of buying wine by the bottle, order by the case. Talk to a wine distributor and compare costs. Wine available in magnums costs less than wine sold by the single bottle. And you will save on corkage fees because there are fewer bottles to open!

Charge everything to one credit card. Have a credit card for the wedding that earns frequent-flyer miles, tracks your expenses and helps pay for your honeymoon. But you must pay the credit card in full every month so you don't run up high-interest debt. Make payments from your designated wedding bank account.

BETTIEQUETTE:
Never ask a friend or family member to perform at a reception—they should be there as a guest, not a provider of free entertainment.

Have a smaller wedding party. Large wedding parties quickly run up bills, with more bouquets, boutonnieres, accessories and thank-you gifts. This really adds up! Keep it intimate to curb costs.

Friends or relatives can contribute their skills or talents instead of boxed gifts. If you know someone with experience in any area that would be useful to you in putting on your wedding, ask them to contribute their expertise instead of a gift. Do you have a friend or relative who could make your wedding cake? Design and print your invitations? Sing or play at the service?

Budget Roundup

Changes in the financing of weddings are altering tradition.
~
Successful planning starts with a preliminary budget.
~
The people signing the checks make the money decisions.
~
The bridal couple makes decisions unrelated to money.
~
Review the many ways to save big bucks.
~
Choose any day but Saturday to save money.
~
Use your friends' talents in lieu of a wedding gift.

The Bridal Budget

Add or delete items as required, then enter your budgeted amount.
Track your actual costs as your planning progresses.

	Your Budget	Actual Cost
Ceremony		
Marriage license	$_____	$_____
Clergy (honorarium)	$_____	$_____
Church/synagogue/temple	$_____	$_____
Musicians	$_____	$_____
Soloist	$_____	$_____
Stationery		
Invitations	$_____	$_____
Reply cards	$_____	$_____
Announcements	$_____	$_____
Thank-you notes	$_____	$_____
Place cards	$_____	$_____
Stamps	$_____	$_____
Guest book	$_____	$_____
Photography & Videography		
Photographer	$_____	$_____
Videographer	$_____	$_____
Transportation & Accommodations		
Limousine or alternative rental	$_____	$_____
Hotel for out-of-town guests	$_____	$_____
Hotel for bride and groom	$_____	$_____
Wedding Cake or Dessert		
Cake	$_____	$_____
Cake knife	$_____	$_____

	Your Budget	Actual Cost
Personal		
Wedding gown	$_____	$_____
Veil and/or headpiece	$_____	$_____
Jewelry	$_____	$_____
Shoes	$_____	$_____
Lingerie	$_____	$_____
Cosmetics	$_____	$_____
Hair stylist	$_____	$_____
Groom's tux/suit rental	$_____	$_____
Flowers		
Bridal bouquet	$_____	$_____
Bridesmaids' bouquets	$_____	$_____
Flowers for the ceremony site	$_____	$_____
Corsages for the family	$_____	$_____
Boutonnieres for the		
groomsmen and family	$_____	$_____
Gifts		
Wedding party gifts	$_____	$_____
Shower hostess gifts	$_____	$_____
Guest favors	$_____	$_____
Grand Total	$_____	$_____

The Reception Budget

Here are two sample budgets,
depending on the venue and whether it will have a cost.
Add or delete items as required, then enter your budgeted amount.
Track your actual costs as your planning progresses.

Reception Budget 1

If you hold the wedding at a hotel or golf club, there likely will
not be a room charge because it is covered by their catering and
bar charges.

	Your Budget	Actual Cost
Venue		
Site rental (if applicable)	$_____	$_____
Punch (15 liters or 4 gallons per 100 guests)	$_____	$_____
Cocktail hour menu	$_____	$_____
Dinner menu (per plate cost x number of guests)	$_____	$_____
Wine (36 bottles per 100 guests)	$_____	$_____
Liquor (18 bottles per 100 guests)	$_____	$_____
Music (DJ or live band)	$_____	$_____
Table centerpieces	$_____	$_____
Gratuities for wait staff (15% of food bill)	$_____	$_____
Grand Total	$_____	$_____

Reception Budget 2

If the site is rented, and you arrange your own catering and bar,
your budget will look like this.

	Your Budget	Actual Cost
Venue		
Site rental	$_____	$_____
Punch (15 liters or 4 gallons per 100 guests)	$_____	$_____

	Your Budget	Actual Cost
Punch glass rental	$_____	$_____
Cocktail hour menu	$_____	$_____
Dinner menu (per plate cost x number of guests)	$_____	$_____
Wine (36 bottles per 100 guests)	$_____	$_____
Wineglass rental	$_____	$_____
Liquor (18 bottles per 100 guests)	$_____	$_____
Liquor glass rental	$_____	$_____
Liquor license (for open bar)	$_____	$_____
Ice (8 bags per 100 guests)	$_____	$_____
Bar mix (65 bottles per 100 guests)	$_____	$_____
Bartender (for 7 hours)	$_____	$_____
Music (DJ or live band)	$_____	$_____
Table centerpieces	$_____	$_____
Gratuities for wait staff (15% of catering—food and wine—bill)	$_____	$_____
Grand Total	$_____	$_____

Make additions
to the ceremony
that reflect your
feelings and your
personalities as
a couple.

Three

The Ceremony

Exchange your vows in an ideal setting

Before you begin to think of all the details involved in planning your service, address all those pesky decisions and legalities, such as obtaining a marriage license and certificate, deciding whether either of you is changing your surname and having a valid passport.

Get your marriage license. Let's back up and review the legalities pertaining to getting married. In many countries, the decision about who gets a license is local. That is, in the United States and Canada, the states and the provinces and territories, respectively, call the shots. Licenses are issued by the county clerk or clerk of the court and you pay a fee. In most jurisdictions you need to show proof of the termination of any prior marriages by divorce, death or annulment, and a couple cannot be

In North America, the states and provinces determine the laws surrounding obtaining marriage licenses.

close relatives. When the license is issued, it usually is valid from one to five days, or up to three months. Occasionally it is open-ended.

Check your passport name and date of expiry. To get a passport in a new name, submit your marriage certificate (the original or a certified copy), identification that carries your signature and your new name, your year of marriage and your spouse's surname.

Start your search for the ceremony and reception sites. With an understanding of the legalities out of the way, concentrate on your search for both the service and reception sites as soon as you become engaged.

The best places book up early. The site for the service may be easy if you have a religious affiliation and will be married in your own church, temple or mosque. Regardless, the booking for the site of the ceremony and then for the reception are the two that you must make first in the planning cycle.

Be flexible. You may have a date and place in mind, but try to be flexible rather than setting your heart on something and be disappointed.

Be original. Find ways to put your own stamp on the ceremony. Examples include writing your vows, choosing special readings or lighting unity candles. Your choice of musicians is personal—perhaps an organist, or a duo playing violin and cello. Some bridal couples choose to have a soloist perform while they sign their marriage certificate.

The point is, make your ceremony reflect the two of you.

Ceremony Choices

Your wedding vows are important, but it's more important to express them in a way that best represents you. These days, engaged couples are inventing their own wedding. Religious? Civil? Traditional? Informal? Solemn? Humorous? These choices allow you to carve out your own day.

Religious Ceremonies

Perhaps your faith is important to you, or maybe you want to honor your family's traditions and values, or you have your heart set on getting married at a particular site.

Get in touch with your church, temple, mosque or synagogue. Find out if your date is available, and also if your pastor, priest, rabbi or pandit is available for that day. Depending on the faith and the requirements of the site, you may have to complete certain programs, such as a pre-marital course (usually three or four sessions), prior to the wedding.

Note that many churches welcome non-members—for a fee. Churches have a number of different fees, depending on your needs. There can be one fee for the use of the church and a separate fee for the clergy, while another fee will include the organist and still another for a small choir. Some religious sites will provide lunch or dinner following a ceremony.

Honor the religious site. There may be specific religious restrictions at the site, such as a dress code. If bare arms are not allowed, wear a small jacket for the service that can be removed for the photography session and reception; if you are required to cover your head, ensure that it works with your gown style. It is likely that confetti or rice will not be allowed in the church or grounds. There may be restrictions on the use of lit candles, the choice of music and the photography during the ceremony. Be clear about the guidelines to avoid last-minute disappointment.

No church? No problem! You can have a religious service even if you are not being married in a church, synagogue or temple. Some retired clergy are glad to have the extra income and they often advertise on their own websites and in bridal magazines. He or she will come to a rehearsal (it's all part of the fee).

Civil Ceremonies

Some bridal couples choose to have an intimate civil ceremony. All you need to be legally married is a civil service officiated by a judge, magistrate, justice of the peace or court clerk. This can solve dilemmas in the case of interfaith unions or make life easier for those marrying a second time. Call your city hall or the marriage bureau for referrals to civil officiants.

Check the laws in your country. In many countries, including Canada, the U.S., the U.K. and India, your license plus your religious service equals a legal marriage. You may be surprised, however, that in some countries only a civil service results in a legal marriage. A religious ceremony is not legally binding, for example, in France, Germany, Austria, Italy, Croatia, Japan or Thailand.

Invite two witnesses. A civil service is twenty minutes, and at the end of it you are presented with a Record of Solemnization. Your permanent marriage certificate can take six to eight weeks to arrive, depending on where you live. Most areas require two witnesses (one for each partner) who must be present at the ceremony. You will also need to have valid photo identification. If you are divorced, you must provide the original or a court-certified copy of the certificate of divorce, final decree or final judgment at the time of booking your ceremony. Photocopies are not accepted.

Choose a small civil service and have a big party to celebrate. It is not unusual for a couple to have a private civil service and then a bang-up reception with all the trimmings with family and friends, so if this is more your speed, go for it.

Commitment Ceremonies

There are only two ways to be legally married: in either a civil or a religious service conducted by a person with the legal authority to conduct weddings. But a commitment service is a popular choice for same-sex couples and those who want to make a public commitment to share their lives but do not want a legal commitment.

Hold an intimate ceremony, without legal commitment. The couple shares vows, usually in front of family and friends. Sometimes a religious commitment service will be in a church, and include hymns and readings and the exchanging of rings—there's just no legal involvement by the state or province. Usually there is a reception that may include toasts, cake cutting, first dance and other wedding traditions.

Negotiating with Your Ceremony Site

Clergy and site fees are non-negotiable. To avoid misunderstandings, ask the right questions:

- What is the site's allowed capacity?
- Are any other weddings scheduled for the same day?
- What is the fee for both the site and the officiant?
- Does the fee include early access so there is time to decorate?
- Does the fee include time for the rehearsal?
- Are any accessories included, such as an aisle runner, flowers or kneeling benches?
- Who sets up the seating for the service?
- What are the restrictions regarding the use of lighted candles, placement of flowers and whether they can be attached at pew ends?

Find out when full payment is due. Do not pay a deposit until the availability of the site or vendor is confirmed.

Choosing an Officiant

Establish the fee upfront. The officiant's fee is based on your relationship with him or her. (For example, your own pastor, from your own church, may not charge you a fee.) This should be a frank discussion. If a fee is charged it may be as low as $100 or as high as $500. Inquire if the cost covers the officiant attending the rehearsal and ask whether he or she would like to attend the wedding reception. (Even if they decline, send an invitation.)

Be clear about details of the service. Discuss whether the officiant intends to give a sermon. If the ceremony is in a different language, will he or she provide a translation?

Inquire what documents the officiant needs to see—and when. When should the marriage license be delivered? If this is a second marriage for either party, will documents be required to show death or divorce that relate to the first marriage? Does the officiant require that the couple complete certain marriage courses before the wedding?

Choose an officiant who shares your values. The wording of the service and the vows should be discussed in detail so there are no surprises the day of the wedding. One of my daughters and her fiancé had an initial discussion with an officiant that revealed his opinion about the role of women within marriage. It differed greatly from that of her and her fiancé. Another couple told of the officiant delivering an unexpected sermon that reflected his values but not theirs.

BETTIEQUETTE:
Make sure in advance that you are comfortable with your choice of officiant—visit, chat, share thoughts and nail down exactly what will be said at the ceremony.

Inform the clergy about your personalized vows. If you choose a religious site, clear every personal element you want to introduce to the service ahead of time, including your own vows, the reading of poems or other material and the type of music. (Some sites may not approve your dancing down the aisle to hard rock!)

Choose officiants familiar with interfaith unions. If two faiths are involved, have a clear vision of how your wedding will accommodate both. Find clergy willing to work together to incorporate both faiths into the service, or choose to have two services. Some couples, if one is Christian and one is Jewish, have one in the church and a second in the synagogue. However, be prepared to answer hard questions from potential officiants, such as whether you have reached an agreement as to the religion in which you'll raise any children.

If you are both inactive in your faiths, you might be married in a Unitarian or civil service.

Troubleshooting Family Issues

Families can be complicated, and issues end up front and center during wedding planning. Approach problems with sensitivity to ensure everyone involved feels comfortable and appreciated.

Give family members time to adjust to your differences. Some families have difficulty accepting disparity in age, different religions, different races or different ethnic backgrounds. No doubt you will have been working on developing acceptance throughout the courting period, but the wedding will raise parents' stress to a new level. Don't expect miracles, or sudden enthusiasm on their part just because you have a ring on your finger. Be understanding and patient. Involving clergy may help to close the gap, helping your parents to recognize your love and easing their misgivings. Remember that both sets of parents just want the best for you and your groom.

Carefully consider decisions relating to divorced parents. Let's start with who will escort the bride down the aisle. A bride may have a father (perhaps whom she rarely sees) and a stepfather with whom she is close. Some outraged fathers have refused to attend a wedding if they are not accorded the honor of escorting their daughter. On the other hand, the bride may want to honor the stepfather who has shared her life from childhood.

Here are some solutions:

Invite both father and stepfather to escort you down the aisle. Sometimes a bride wants to honor her stepfather, but doesn't want to hurt her father's feelings. in this case, she may be escorted by both men—assuming they are friendly with each other and not insulted by being asked to share the honor! Ask your father to escort you halfway down the aisle, where you will be joined by your stepfather. There are two ways to conclude this exchange: both your father and stepfather can continue to the altar with you, or your birth father can slip into his pew while your stepfather continues to the altar and then steps back into his pew.

Be escorted by both parents. In some religions this is standard and it is a lovely way to honor your mother. (Note, though, that this can crowd the aisle and interfere with the impact of the bride's entrance if she is wearing a full-skirted gown. It is, after all, the bride's big moment.) If a bride is close to her mother, however, and willing to share her triumphant march to the altar, it is an unselfish and lovely gesture.

Go to the altar unescorted. This option comes as a surprise to some but, as one bride said, "If I have to be escorted by my father, my fiancé has to be escorted by his mother. I'm an adult, for Pete's sake." So walking alone is an option for many women. This can be charming if the groom walks toward his bride, meets her at the halfway mark, and together they approach the altar. (This is a happy solution when there are hard feelings about who will win the father/stepfather war.) Both of my own daughters preferred to join their fiancés halfway down the aisle. My daughter-in-law, who is more traditional, was escorted by her father.

All of these options are suggestions. It is always the bride's personal choice how she will make this short but important journey.

Acknowledge the mother-of-the-bride in a dramatic, but practical way. In a church wedding, the bride's mother is the last person seated. After she is seated, there is sometimes a gap of a few minutes before the processional begins. That gap can be closed so that the mother actually becomes part of the processional.

Here's how: The mother-of-the-bride is escorted to the first pew by one of the ushers. Her moving down the aisle sends the signal to the organist (or harpist or whoever is providing the music) to stop playing. The sudden silence will draw attention to the fact that something is about to happen. Just before the mother reaches the pew, the music for the processional begins. Mother does not sit down, but remains standing and turns, facing the rear of the church. Her standing, the processional music and the start down the aisle of the first attendant is the signal for everyone else to rise. All is underway. The mother has had her unique moment in the sun, and the attention now focuses on her daughter.

Don't allow the groom's parents to feel left out. Once upon a time the bride's parents paid for the wedding and the groom's parents were just honored guests. But those days are gone, so find ways to honor the groom's family during the service. For example, invite them to light a unity candle during the ceremony.

BETTIEQUETTE:

Tuck two tiny bouquets into your larger bouquet. As you near the altar, pause and present a mini-bouquet to each of the mothers. It is a charming way of honoring them equally, and watchful guests will silently applaud you.

Reserve that front pew for the mother-of-the-bride. It may be that when parents are divorced the father is picking up the tab—perhaps with his new wife. Regardless of who is paying the bills, the bride's mother retains the preferential seating in the first pew. The father and his wife will sit in either the second or the third pew. If the mother is unmarried she can sit alone, sit with a member of the family or invite a friend (of either sex) to sit with her. That person would be seated before the mother is seated.

The Processional and Recessional

The magic moment is when you walk down the aisle, and the triumphant moment is when you make the return trip!

Accept the rules and limitations of the religious site. Some churches have very strict guidelines. Don't ignore these, for example, on the assumption that the clergy won't interrupt a service to halt an aggressive photographer. You may be in for a surprise!

Follow tradition if you have a religious processional. In many Christian services, the groomsmen enter before the processional and wait at the altar. Often they lead the processional, and occasionally they escort the bridesmaids down the aisle.

The processional begins as soon as the bride's mother is escorted to the first pew. After the groomsmen are at the front of the church, next come the bridesmaids, the maid of honor (best woman), the flower girl or ring bearer, then the bride, walking alone, to the left of her escort or flanked by both parents.

In Hindu ceremonies, the bride's maternal uncle and his wife escort the bride to the altar.

A Jewish processional is led by the rabbi or cantor, then the grandparents of the groom, the grandparents of the bride, the groomsmen (in pairs), the groom and his parents (dad on the left, mom on the right), the bridesmaids, the maid of honor, the flower girl or ring bearer, the bride and her parents (dad on the left, mom on the right).

Follow long-established traditions for a recessional. The Christian recessional is led by the bride and groom. They are followed by the flower girl or ring bearer (unless they have been sitting with their parents), the honor attendants, and the bridesmaids and groomsmen in pairs, followed by the bride's parents, the groom's parents and then the guests.

The Jewish recessional is led by the bridal couple followed by the bride's parents and groom's parents. Then the flower girl and ring bearer, male and female honor attendants together, bridesmaids and groomsmen in pairs, cantor, and finally the rabbi.

If there are more female than male attendants, have the best woman walk alone. These days, there are often more bridesmaids than ushers. The maid of honor may walk alone or, depending on the numbers, two bridesmaids may walk together, followed by the other maids and ushers in pairs.

Meet with the musician(s) about choices and options. Do your homework before this meeting. Check iTunes for wedding music albums if you don't already have music in mind. Music should be played thirty minutes before the service begins and during both the processional and the recessional.

Create ceremony programs. Programs are an effective way to acknowledge participants in the service, including the officiant, musician(s), those doing special readings and your attendants.

Involve guests in the ceremony with a candle lighting. The guests are each given a candle when they arrive. During the ceremony, the parents each light side candles at the altar. The bridal couple takes these two candles to light the center candle. They then take the center candle and lights the candle of the person sitting at the end of each pew. Each guest with a lighted candle turns and lights the candle of the person beside them, and so on along the pew. When all the candles are lit, the officiant gives a benediction.

The Rehearsal

An organized rehearsal is essential to the success of your wedding ceremony. Many people have it the night before the wedding, but if all of the attendants live locally, plan to have the rehearsal a few days before the wedding.

Rehearse the ushers. In a formal wedding, an usher will ask a couple upon their arrival if they are guests of the bride or the groom. Then they will offer their arm to the woman and the male guest will follow behind. The bride's guests will be seated at one side of the aisle and the groom's guests grouped at the other side. If one side has many more guests than the other, it is best to mix the seating (always reserving the front pews for the parents). In a less formal wedding, it is entirely appropriate to seat guests on either side of the aisle. Ushers can greet the guests at the door, give them a ceremony program and invite them to seat themselves.

BETTIEQUETTE:
The process for seating guests on wedding day should be established at the rehearsal.

Don't invite anyone except the wedding party and the parents to the rehearsal. Having too many people at the rehearsal is disruptive and it turns the event into a party, much to the irritation of the clergy. The participants should include only the bridal couple, the parents of the bride and groom, the service officiant, the wedding party, and the ring bearers and flower girls and their parents.

The Rehearsal Dinner

The rehearsal dinner can be co-hosted. The rehearsal dinner was once hosted by the groom's parents only, but today it's not necessarily their responsibility. If they are co-hosting the wedding, the hosting of the rehearsal dinner can be shared, too. Here are some options:

- One set of parents may have it at their home, while the other parents may offer to bring libations and dessert.
- Both sets of parents may co-host the dinner at a restaurant.
- The bridal couple may host the event as a way of saying thank you to their parents and attendants for supporting them throughout the planning of the wedding.

Invite close relatives and out-of-town guests to the rehearsal dinner. It's thoughtful to include relatives and out-of-town guests to the rehearsal dinner. They would not, however, be invited to the rehearsal. Additional guests at the dinner should include the following:

- Attendants' spouses or dates
- Family members who are not in the wedding party
- Grandparents
- People singing or giving a reading

The site for the rehearsal dinner may be a restaurant, club or private home. If it is a summer wedding, go for an informal supper in a garden. Private golf and yacht clubs are popular venues.

Order a pre-set menu if the dinner is held in a restaurant or club. You can place the order ahead of time so that no menus are presented, just as if you were entertaining in your own home.

Arrange a buffet if the dinner is held at home. When held at home, the dinner is an informal event and a buffet is conducive to relaxation, mingling, storytelling and fun.

Keep the home menu simple so there is no stress on the hosts. Choose a menu of dishes that can be prepared ahead of time. Set up a self-serve wine bar. Have a small decorated cake so the bridal couple can cut it together while guests toast them.

Make sure everyone is in the know. The secret to planning a smooth service is to share all relevant guidelines with everyone involved at the rehearsal dinner. This includes the smallest of details:

- Who will conduct the service?
- Who is responsible for paying and delivering the officiant fee?
- What limitations have been set by the site?
- Has the clergy approved additions to the service?
- Where will the male attendants gather before the service?
- Will the boutonnieres be delivered to the men at the service site?
- What time will music begin prior to the service?
- What music has been chosen for each part of the wedding?

By the time the rehearsal is over, everyone should be clear about their own responsibilities and expectations.

Ceremony Roundup

Make a contribution to the service to make it your own.

~

Come to an agreement about what the clergy will say.

~

Get clergy approval of your vows.

~

Find clergy, if needed, for an interfaith marriage.

~

Ask if the site provides an organist, singer or choir.

~

Ask if the site can provide runner, pew ends, candles.

Pick a venue that is perfect for you and perfect for your guests.

Four

The Reception

Welcome to the biggest party you will ever give

The spiritual and emotional commitment that is central to the marital ceremony moves on to your party of parties. It's celebration time! You will never again have a day in which your emotions run from spiritual to bang-up fun in such a short time. What a trip!

The first item on your agenda is to decide where the ceremony will be held. Once you know that, it's time to find a reception venue. If you have a clear idea of both locations, you may be surprised to discover how far ahead they need to be booked. So decide on a site as soon as you can. Only then can you plan the details of your wedding.

When each decision is made, don't revisit it. Let it go. This may be the most important advice in this book: Looking back and wondering if you could have made better choices will drive you crazy. Make your decisions and move on.

BETTIEQUETTE:

Take a relaxed attitude of "Who cares? I'm having a wonderful day and nothing is going to upset me." That's the route to a successful wedding.

Know that things _will_ go wrong. On your big day, important events may run pretty smoothly, but the devil is in the details. Some aspects will not proceed exactly as you had envisioned. Don't let anything get to you. A pouting or distraught bride is a huge negative for family and guests.

Choosing the Site

Which reception venue to use is a huge decision because it's the bedrock of the party and can determine its success. If you're going to shop around, move ahead in an organized way—step by logical step.

The search for the reception site starts with intensive homework. (What a surprise!) Move quickly and efficiently, because the popular venues are booked not only months ahead, but sometimes more than a year in advance. If you have your heart set on a specific location, in some ways, it makes things easier. On the downside, if it's _your_ favorite place, you can bet it is the preferred choice of a whole lot of other couples too!

Take into account the size of the wedding. Choose a site that suits the size of your wedding. An intimate wedding with forty to fifty guests gets lost in a cathedral, but would be perfect in a chapel.

Hold the wedding service and reception under one roof for the convenience of guests. If you aren't being married in a church, temple or synagogue, get on your computer and check out large hotels, small inns and a variety of other options that can handle both events. Follow up on those that look promising with a phone call and make notes while you're chatting.

Consider art galleries, museums and other historical sites. Choose an imaginative setting. Many of these places have discovered that hosting weddings can be a source of revenue. Each of these special sites will have its own guidelines, so ask lots of questions.

- Will they provide a short list of caterers they find acceptable?
- Are they equipped to provide tables, chairs, tableware and linens? (If not, be prepared to arrange for rentals, including delivery and pickup.)
- Will they limit the hours the site will be available to you? (If so, don't count on a reception that will evolve into an early-morning bash.)
- Will they require you to take out a one-day insurance policy to cover possible damage to their valuables?
- Will they require payment for providing their own guard or supervisor?

Many large and lovely houses are available for weddings. Grand houses are increasingly popular and provide a gracious setting for your vows. They are often surrounded by beautiful grounds, so, weather permitting, you may be able to hold an outdoor service in the gardens followed by an indoor reception. You will find these on the Web.

Work closely with the site in your planning. Communicate with the managers—and don't think you can plan any extraordinary activity without their approval. One bridal couple held their wedding in a historic home and spent a fortune on clustering very expensive candles on each table, but after the tables were set on the wedding day they were told the candles could not be lit. This restriction is common in older locations where an open flame is a no-no.

Plan an outdoor service in a public park. Remember that you need to obtain written permission, get a food and drink license, perhaps arrange for lighting, and often make arrangements for portable potties. You also need a backup plan in case of rain. It seems easy to plan a small, casual wedding in a public park, but these can be the most difficult sites of all with which to work.

Be flexible about your wedding date. If your desired location is a must-have, decide with your partner and your family on three acceptable wedding dates before you meet with the venue manager. The more popular the location, the heavier the bookings, so it can make all the difference if you have alternative dates to suggest.

Talk to married friends and review their experiences. The best advertising is word of mouth. Your friends will gladly tell you the pros and cons of their own experiences. Then, with a shorter list in hand, you can decide which venue most appeals to you.

Check out the advertising in bridal magazines. Ads tell their story succinctly and a picture will give you a sense of the venue's ambience. You can cut out a magazine ad and put it in your workbook. Ads occasionally provide sample menus and even a price range. Pull up venues on the Web as well; print a small selection and add these to your notes.

Make direct contact with a few sites that interest you. Finally! With your short list in hand, start accumulating information from the comfort of home. Phone or email the venues, and ask basic questions, especially about date availability, before you visit. Why waste your time with a personal visit if the dates you want aren't open?

Ask for a range of menu costs. Hotels, private clubs and restaurants provide catering. Any cost given over the phone will be based on their basic menus. This is just a starting point. Be aware that as you build the cocktail party and dinner menus, you inevitably will want extras.
    Galleries, museums, some banquet halls and historic homes often

leave the catering to you. They may, however, allow only specific caterers, so ask for their approved list.

Ask how bar costs are handled. People today generally drink less alcohol at weddings than they did just a few years ago. Awareness of the dangers of drinking and driving has had an impact.

Lower alcohol consumption in turn has encouraged many caterers and reception sites to offer a price that includes bar, which helps bridal couples with their budget. If the bar costs are separate, ask for specifics. It may be calculated per drink, or based on bottles used, or in some facilities you may be able to provide your own liquor and pay a corkage fee.

At one time, bar costs were at least as high as food costs.

Know the site restrictions. There are horror stories of guests standing outside in the rain because they were denied access to the site until a specific time. Does the venue allow early access to decorate? At what hour must the party end? Are candles permitted?

Ask how many other weddings may be booked on your day. Banquet halls are often set up to accommodate two or more weddings at one time. How will your guests be directed to your ballroom? Is there a separate entrance for each ballroom? Are there separate areas for a pre-dinner cocktail party? How good is the soundproofing? Will music from an adjacent ballroom intrude on your space?

Don't forget about guest parking. Rural and suburban hotels likely have free parking for your guests, but major city hotels will not. See if a system can be set up so the hosts pay your guests' parking.

Narrow the list to no more than two or three locations and visit each. Arrive with an even more specific list of questions. See the next page for some suggestions.

Questions to Ask the Reception Site

What are the site restrictions? Be sure that you know of any limitations, and get these in writing.

What are the available menu options? Review specific options for the cocktail party, the dinner, and perhaps a late-night dessert table. Get exact costs, including any extras you may want.

How many servers are provided? The ratio will be based on the size of your guest list. For a formal multi-course dinner, you want one server per ten to twelve guests. For a meal with only three courses (appetizer, entrée, dessert), one waiter per twenty-five guests is adequate. At a cocktail party, you need one bartender for fifty to seventy-five guests, plus waiters to circulate with trays of hors d'oeuvres.

What types of food services are available? Do you have the option of table service, buffet or family-style (when platters of food are delivered to the table for sharing)?

Does the venue provide linens for the event? Or do you arrange your own tablecloth and napkin rentals? Does the venue offer sheer overlays? Table centers?

How is tipping handled? Do they add a surcharge to cover the tipping? If so, what percentage? Who is tipped? Servers? Bartender? Kitchen staff?

Is there a separate area available for smokers? The dining room will likely not allow smoking, so there should be an adjacent outdoor area provided. If this is not offered, you may find some guests sneaking out for a smoke, or leaving early!

It was not so long ago that imprinted matchbooks were on each guest's table. How times have changed!

How large and how convenient are the washrooms? How far away are the washrooms from the cocktail and dining area? How many stalls are in each? Are they adequate for the number of guests you have invited?

Will the site cooperate with your vendors? Be clear about the specific time your wedding consultant, florist, band, DJ and caterer can access your venue for setting up . . . and get the venue's agreement in writing. You don't want to rely on your memory. (Are you rolling your eyes at the number of times I say "Get it in writing"? Trust me. It's a message that deserves repetition.)

Is there a tasting visit? A venue that has its own kitchen and is proud of its cuisine will usually invite you to sample their food before you make a commitment. Take advantage of this to ensure you know your options and are happy with the quality of the food (and the price!).

Review your notes before you leave. Know exactly what was covered, including if they do the catering and how much flexibility there is within each menu. Know what the prices are for extras you're considering. And know what extra charges may be involved for service, gratuities, cleanup and staff for the parking lot. (At most reputable sites, the extra charge will just be for the gratuity.) Ask for any printed literature they have about their services.

BETTIEQUETTE:

Beware of the manager who seems offended by your questions and your insistence on wanting the details in writing.

Sign a contract that spells out every detail. A signed contract is the only firm commitment that confirms your date. Verbal promises are not binding, and the venue could be scooped up by another couple in a blink of an eye. The manager of a reliable venue will be pleased that you want everything spelled out in detail. This clarifies your expectations and protects both parties.

Plan Your Reception

When planning the details of your reception, have your guests top of mind.

Put the comfort and enjoyment of your guests above all else. Consider their comfort, the age spread, their tastes in food, convenience of parking for older guests and transportation for out-of-town guests.

Offer food throughout the cocktail hour. Serve interesting canapés with tray service or have a food station with finger foods.

Prepare a seating plan. A well-planned reception involves sensitive seating arrangements that place compatible guests together. This may turn out to be the most challenging of all your wedding chores!

Turn to your parents for advice about guests of their generation. Both sets of parents can help you avoid seating that will make anyone feel uncomfortable.

Showcase Your Seating

Seating chart. This should be in alphabetical order and placed at the entrance to the dining room. The chart indicates the table, but at the table guests may choose their own seat.

Place cards. These are placed on the table and indicate the specific seat for each guest. If guests require special meals because of diet restrictions, specific seating helps the server deliver each dish to the appropriate person.

Numbered tables. An alternative is to give a number or name to each table. It's interesting, for example, to come up with a theme for your table names, such as your favorite travel destinations.

BETTISQUETTE.
Traditional seating dictates that the head table be at the top of the room, but this setup means tables at the back of the space are some distance from the bridal couple. To avoid this disconnect, consider a head table in the center of the room.

The no seating-plan event. If you and your groom are planning for a very casual, relaxed wedding, skip the seating plan. Allow guests to choose where they want to sit.

Decide where the bridal couple will sit. The bridal couple (and often the entire wedding party) sits at the head table, usually a long rectangle at the top of the room, sometimes elevated. Some couples, however, opt for a "sweetheart table" for just the two of them in the center of the room. Their attendants would be seated at another table with their escorts. Increasingly popular is a large round table in the center of the room that accommodates the entire bridal party and ensures that no guests are seated out in the wilderness, far away from the happy couple.

Choose music that sets the right mood for the service and reception. Budget for music that will set the right mood for both events. You will pay extra if you want the church musician(s) at the rehearsal, but most professionals who regularly play for weddings won't feel their attendance at the rehearsal is necessary. A private meeting in advance with the musicians will help you sort out the options. For music at the reception, you may choose a DJ or a live band.

Make your first dance as husband and wife memorable. The bridal couple may choose to make an extended ceremony of the first-dance event. If so, after you dance together and then with your parents, you may ask the bridesmaids and groomsmen to pair off and dance together before all the guests are invited to join you on the dance floor.

Your big day can be an emotional mine field or one of euphoria. And you won't be surprised to know that the key is—you guessed it—detailed planning. There are myriad questions to be asked and details to be remembered, so keep notes. You'll be glad you did.

Reception Roundup

Be flexible about your date to get the site you want.

~

Do your initial shopping in a bridal magazine and on the Web.

~

Visit no more than three potential locations.

~

Ask the venue all the necessary questions.

~

Familiarize yourself with site restrictions and regulations.

~

Get the lowdown on any extra costs.

~

Factor in tipping, but don't tip twice!

~

Check that the contract you're signing spells out all the details.

It starts with finding the right bridal gown. All other fashion choices relate to the style of the bride.

Five

Wedding Fashion

Go for the big wow on your big day

Whatever your personal style, there's a perfect gown out there waiting for you. You just have to find each other!

A word of advice before you start shopping: don't limit your style options. Certainly have a sense of what you'd like to wear (wedding magazines are perfect for research), but shop with an open mind and don't dismiss the salesperson's suggestions. Boutique advisers say that it is surprising how many brides, after choosing their gown, say, "I wouldn't have imagined that this style would be right for me. I'm so glad you persuaded me to try it on." What works for your regular wardrobe may not work at all in a wedding gown.

Don't take a group gown shopping with you. Shop with one person, someone whose taste you trust. That will save you dealing with the

BETTIEQUETTE:

Never go shopping with more than one person. Trust me— you will end up buying a gown that pleases everyone but yourself.

opinions and ideas of a whole peanut gallery. An experienced salesperson will size up your body type and take into account the size and site of your wedding, as well as your budget. She can also be your advocate if you have friends accompanying you who have far too much to say!

Invite your mother to shop with you for your gown. Your mother, in fact, may be the best person to accompany you as you search for a gown. Mothers have no agenda beyond wanting their daughters to be lovely on their wedding day—you'll get the best advice from her.

Start gown shopping early. Start shopping for your gown at least nine months before the wedding because it may take five to seven months to get delivery. I advise giving your boutique an early delivery date to allow for possible delays, as well as alterations. These days most gowns are made overseas, so it's important to start shopping early! If you don't have the luxury of time, buy off-the-rack. Most boutiques carry a range of styles and sizes as well as their own made-to-order sample dresses.

Boutiques are a reliable place to shop for your gown. Your best bet is to visit a well-established retailer that specializes in bridal fashion. They carry a variety of lines and provide customized service, limiting the possibility of disappointment. Check with the store to see if they do alterations, and how much they charge.

Stay offline when it comes to gown shopping. Be careful about shopping online for gowns, especially those made in East Asia. Established designers warn that their gowns are being copied—even their names are used—in inferior fabric and with shoddy workman-ship. With these counterfeit lines you run the risk of getting the wrong gown and/or late delivery (and if this happens, you would have no recourse).

Schedule fittings to get the dress size you need. If you are a plus size, phone the retailers in your area to see if they carry sample dresses in plus sizes. This way you won't look at a size six and imagine it on your body! Measurements matter more than size.

Bridal sizes are not a match for your usual size. A size ten in an everyday dress may be a size twelve or fourteen in bridal. Therefore, it's important to not rely on the number on the tag, and to schedule proper visits for measurements and fittings.

Be prepared to pay a deposit for your dress. When you place your custom dress order, you will be asked for a deposit. A non-refundable deposit of fifty percent is generally required. Put the deposit on a credit card in case something goes amiss or the store goes out of business. This shows proof of purchase and increases the chance you will get your deposit back. Also request a hard-copy receipt with the style number, size, color and date of delivery.

Ask about the store's refund policy. Make sure you know what the policy is if the manufac-turer can't deliver your dress on time. If you have invested in a wedding insurance policy (through your insurance agency), consider protection for your dress. You can get a policy that covers the safe delivery of your dress. This will protect you against something unforeseen, like a store closing.

BETTIEQUETTE:
Never buy or order a gown a size smaller because you plan to lose weight. It is possible to have a gown made smaller, but almost impossible to make it larger.

Select styles to suit the site and season. Where and when you have your wedding is your style guide. Below are a few guidelines, but ignore them if they don't match your vision. After all, it's your day and your dream.

When:

Spring and Summer. Look at lightweight fabrics that breathe, such as lightweight silks, eyelet, chiffon, organza, charmeuse, silk shantung and tulle.

Fall and Winter. This invites lush fabrics with more ornate embellishments, brocade, heavier silk, velvet, matte jersey, satins, and heavier lace such as Battenberg.

Where:

Beach. Choose an unadorned, gauzy gown that seems to float.

Barn. Acknowledge your surroundings with a simple style, perhaps an A-line. Consider a short dress.

Garden or park. Choose a gown that does not touch the ground—and especially avoid a train or long veil. These catch on the grass as you "walk down the aisle." The outdoor surroundings call out for color, so introduce a splash in a belt, shoes, jewelry, shrug, or shawl.

Art gallery or museum. Once again, your surroundings offer an invitation and in this instance it is to be sophisticated and understated. Be the last word in chic.

Historic house. Go vintage-inspired. Think Victorian era. Think lace.

Ballroom. Go full out in a grand ballroom gown with a train.

Pick the Style of Your Dress with Care

The style you choose should be figure flattering. Don't copy the style of your favorite celebrity. Be inspired, but zero in on what's best for your specific body type.

Standard Shapes

Ballroom. The full skirt disguises the hips and puts the emphasis on the bodice, making it ideal for women with larger hips.

Sheath. This style has a simple, narrow line that works well for the slim woman with small breasts.

Empire. This shape is similar to the sheath, but the bodice line is just under the breast.

Mermaid. This style is popular and needs a great body. It hugs the figure and then flares from below the knee.

A-line. This shape has a gently flared skirt that flatters most body types.

Fit-and-flare. A newer style, the shape of this dress has a fitted bodice, with a skirt that flares from the hip.

Drop waist. The flare on this style starts even higher than the fit-and-flare, at the hip bone.

Ballroom

Sheath

Empire

Mermaid

A-line

Drop Waist

Fit-and-Flare

Veiled Hints

A veil is not a requirement, but it adds to the overall impact of the dress. The style of the veil depends on the formality of both the gown and the wedding, the size of the wedding and the site of the service.

Birdcage or Flyaway. These veils cover the face. The birdcage is tight over the face and the flyaway is loose, but both are very short. They are chic options, and ideal for the bride who is shy or nervous and will feel more comfortable if she is less exposed.

Blusher or Fountain. These are both short veils that fall just below the shoulder. The blusher has a shorter overlay that pulls over the face. These are ideal with a short gown or for a less formal wedding.

Elbow or Waterfall. Both of these styles are waist length and may have two layers. They are shorter at the front and taper to the waist at the back and usually attach at the back of the head. They are ideal for less formal weddings.

Fingertip or Waltz. Hold your arms straight down and the length is to the tip of your fingers. It may have a shorter overlay for volume. This is a graceful length that doesn't interfere with walking.

Floor Length. This veil is dramatic. It usually attaches at the back of the head and is feminine as well as formal, but because it doesn't have a train it makes walking easy.

Chapel. Attaching at the back of the head and sweeping into a train, the chapel veil is formal. Like the mantilla, it is effective in creating drama during the walk down the aisle and presents a pretty picture when the bride stands at the altar.

Mantilla. This is a traditional Spanish veil with a wide edging all around. It is about the same length as the chapel veil. It sits well forward on the head and has a slight train. Ornate and lovely.

Cathedral. This is the most dramatic of all veils and is generally worn in a cathedral or other large place of worship. It is very long (an indeterminate length) and only worn at large, formal weddings.

Blusher or Fountain

Birdcage or Flyaway

Elbow or
Waterfall

Fingertip
or Waltz

Chapel

Floor Length

Mantilla

Cathedral

Alternative Headpieces

Your choice of headpiece will depend on how you wear your hair. If you have long hair and it's already your crowning glory, choose a subtle, small-scale hair accessory. If, however, you plan to sweep your hair into a sophisticated updo or pull it back into a chignon, you can ramp up the glamour.

Tiaras. These are still a time-tested and popular option and they combine well with a veil. The veil can be removed at the reception and the tiara works nicely on its own.

Fascinators. These can be as elaborate as the hairstyle will allow and are an increasingly popular option.

Fresh flowers. You might tuck a large one, such as a lily or orchid, at the nape of the neck. Or you may group together smaller flowers, like tiny rosebuds or daisies. These flowers are good choices because they last for many hours without wilting.

Faux flowers. Deliberately designed to look fake, a large fabric flower might have crystals sparkling in the center or on the rim of each petal. These elaborate headpieces make a dramatic statement.

Feathers. These make a graceful addition, creating slight movement.

Jeweled clips and combs. When hair is worn long and full, these adornments can be a subtle and beautiful addition.

Bring On the Bling!

Your gown and veil are just the beginning. Now, consider the accessories to complete your look.

When it comes to accessories, less is more. Wearing only one major piece of jewelry rather than several pieces makes a stronger statement. Large earrings and a necklace cancel each other out, so pick one or the other. However, if your arms are bare, a bracelet or wide cuff is a nice addition.

Keep your tissues close by. A small bag can be reassuring for the bride who wants to have tissues and cosmetics close at hand. There are beautiful jeweled clutches available, but a small fabric pouch with a drawstring that will slip over the wrist is also a practical choice.

Shoes

Choose heels that suit your style and comfort level. Sky-high heels add to stature if you can walk well in them, but think of all the celebrities you have seen on talk shows or at awards ceremonies, stumbling on stage in heels they can't handle. An elegant, confident walk trumps high-heel awkwardness every time.

A shoe with a mid-heel may be a better choice if you haven't mastered high heels. If you're tying the knot on a beach, you may want to go barefoot. Cowboy boots in an informal setting, such as a barn, are fun. And some brides provide flip-flops for their guests so they can get down and dirty when the dancing heats up.

For happy feet, consider two pairs of shoes. Comfort counts; the higher heel is great for the service and the photography, but your feet will thank you if you change into comfortable low heels or flats for dancing. (They will thank you even more if long before your wedding day you've worn your high heels around the house and broken them in.)

Show off with color. Shoes are usually white or cream, but brides with a sense of fun sometimes wear a bright color. Just because!

Bridesmaids' Fashion

Today, bridesmaids pay for their own dress and shoes, which has resulted in a subtle shift in the decision-making.

Years ago, the bride's father paid for the bridesmaids' dresses. This gave the bride total control over what her attendants wore.

Treat dress choice as a collaboration. It's important that you work with your bridesmaids to establish a style that pleases them while emphasizing the overall style of the wedding. The bride chooses the color and length and that becomes the common denominator. It is a bonus if the bridesmaids can collectively agree on the style.

Let your bridesmaids determine their style. Today, bridesmaids seldom dress exactly alike. Increasingly each chooses her own style within the color and length parameters. Women know what works best for them and their individual figures. Allow your bridesmaids the freedom to choose their own dress. Think of it as an extra gift to them.

Keep the shoe style similar. While dresses may be slightly different, shoes should be similar. Either all should wear the closed pump or all should wear the open sandal. Or if the wedding's on a beach, allow everyone to go barefoot.

BETTIEQUETTE:
The bridesmaids do not pay for any extras that the bride wants them to wear. This includes hats, gloves, and of course, the bouquets they will carry. Because the bride chooses these accessories, the costs are her obligation.

Have your bridesmaids schedule their own fitting appointments. If ordered through a bridal boutique, dresses are ordered by size but adjusted to fit after they arrive. The bridesmaid can get a price for a one-time fitting/adjustment. Each bridesmaid can make her own arrangement for paying for both the gown and the fitting. Bridesmaids should be careful not to order a size that is too small. They should order by body measurements rather than a pre conceived style number.

Accept a bridesmaid's resignation with grace. Sometimes a bridesmaid becomes overwhelmed by the financial cost of taking part. It is acceptable for her to step down. She should speak up sooner rather than later, and the bride should accept her decision with understanding. Perhaps the former bridesmaid can be offered another way to participate in the wedding.

Encourage mothers of the bridal couple to talk about their dress choices. The mothers of the bride and groom will make their own choices. However, it's a good idea for them to be in touch so they can select colors that will complement each other in the wedding pictures, but avoid the same color. The mother-of-the-bride gets first choice.

The Groom's Wedding Day Fashion

Grooms should check out the traditional options and then decide to follow, bend or break the rules. His choice, however, should take into account what the bride is wearing and the size and formality of the wedding. From there, it's about his personal style.

Have male attendants pay for their own suits. As with the bridesmaids, groomsmen are responsible for the cost of their wedding day attire. They may wear their own tuxedos, but if tuxedos are being rented, payment is their obligation. They should make themselves available for being measured and for a separate fitting, and they are responsible for picking up and returning the rental. The rental ensemble will include the suit, shirt and studs, tie, vest or cummerbund, and often shoes.

Formal Groomswear

The man of the day has a few options to choose from—depending on what his bride is wearing, of course! The most formal attire is white tie. The jacket is black, with tails, and worn with a white vest and a bow tie. Black tie is less formal. A tuxedo is worn with a bow tie and, traditionally, a cummerbund. Today, a cummerbund is often replaced with a vest, and a Windsor or four-in-hand tie is often worn instead of the bow tie.

Shirts. Either the wing or turned-down collar is appropriate with tuxedos. However, wing-collar shirts are a must with full dress "tails" and with the cutaway when an ascot is worn. The formal shirt is closed with studs and the cuff closes with cuff links.

Shoes. Oxfords are the most popular today, replacing the traditional opera slippers. Patent leather is suggested (but not mandatory) for formal weddings.

Pocket square. The shape and size of a pocket square become the punctuation mark of formal dress. Are you going to finish with a period or an exclamation point? Listen to the advice of the expert who is helping coordinate your formalwear—he or she can help coordinate color and print.

Vest or cummerbund. Vests are popular today. The color and pattern might coordinate with, but not necessarily match, the bridesmaids' dresses. Today, the cummerbund is not as popular but it provides a good-looking accent.

Boutonniere. It is a nice touch if the groom's boutonniere is not a match with those worn by his attendants. It is a sentimental choice if it repeats a flower in the bride's bouquet. Consider everything from seasonal flowers to fern and thistles.

Informal Groomswear

The occasion may call for "black tie optional," and this gives the groom, his attendants and the guests the option of wearing a tuxedo or a dark suit. The choice for a garden wedding or a wedding in an informal setting, such as a barn, can be more relaxed. A casual jacket and shirt, with or without a tie, is just fine, as long as the bride has also made a casual choice.

Dress for a beach wedding can range in formality. It may be totally casual, but if the bride chooses to wear a long white wedding gown, the groom needs at least a crisp white shirt with a collar and well-tailored pants, perhaps in white, tan or black linen.

For everyone involved in a wedding, fashion is about personal style. Even for Dad, who may struggle to button the jacket of that tux he hasn't worn in years. (And hold your breath that the pant seams won't split when he sits down.) These guidelines are meant to be helpful, but what matters most is that the bridal couple can agree on the overall style of the wedding.

Fashion Roundup

Rely on the expertise and experience of your boutique.

~

Begin gown shopping nine months before your wedding day.

~

Choose a style that fits the venue.

~

Fabric choice will depend on the season.

~

Beware of shopping online for a bargain.

~

Let your bridesmaids' personal styles shine through.

~

The groom takes his cue from the bride when it comes to what he wears.

Don't be in a hurry to choose your attendants. There often is a trade-off between family and friends.

Six

The Wedding Party

Carefully choose who will share your big day with you

I n most cases there is some time between your engagement and wedding, so don't be in a hurry to decide on your wedding party.

Decide on the size of your wedding first. The number of attendants depends on the size of the wedding. A large wedding often has more attendants. If the bridal couple decides on a small wedding, more than one attendant each may be overkill.

Take into account the location. Where the wedding will be held is a factor in deciding the number of attendants. Will it be a destination wedding on a beach? This will mean travel expenses for your attendants and may make it financially out of reach for some. Are you returning to your parents' hometown for the wedding where you will be surrounded by people you grew up with but now rarely see, making it a larger wedding?

Start by making a list of all potential attendants. Put a notation beside each name regarding why they would be suitable. Consider choices that would please your parents, please your groom's family and, of course, please yourself. Don't make a final decision until you examine all the possibilities and their ramifications for you and various family members, siblings and friends. This is not a good time to be impulsive. Decisions about who is to be in the wedding party can become highly political.

Choose a sister or a close friend to be your maid of honor. This decision not only has an impact on your wedding, but also affects the months of planning preceding the big day. Perhaps you share all your joys and your problems with your best friend and are not close to your sister. But what if your mother is quick to remind you that blood is thicker than water and, anyway, what will the extended family think if you snub your sister? One option is to have two maids of honor, and they can share the privilege and responsibilities. There are no easy answers here; much depends on your family dynamic. But give careful thought to your decision.

Consider relatives when you choose your attendants. Perhaps it's a given that your sister will be your maid of honor, but it may be wise to include your fiancé's sister or a cousin that you always liked as an attendant. These people are likely to be in your life for *all* your life, even if you don't often see them. Ask yourself who you are mostly likely to still be in touch with ten or twenty years down the road.

Be prepared that friends may turn down your invitation to be an attendant. While most women love being part of the excitement that leads up to a wedding, not all do. Perhaps they can't afford the honor; the financial or time investment may be too much. Sometimes a friend is self-conscious and prefers to avoid that sort of spotlight. Be gracious about this and don't take it personally. If it is a close friend that you want to be involved in your special day, find another way for her or him to participate.

Here Come the Women: The Bridesmaids

Be aware of the financial cost for your bridesmaids. The bridesmaids usually pay for their own dresses, shoes and jewelry. They also take care of their own makeup and hair.

Reduce the financial obligation of your wedding party whenever possible. In addition to their dresses, the financial cost for attendants may involve a wedding gift plus a gift for each shower—not to mention the expense of bachelor and bachelorette parties. This can be costly, so encourage your bridesmaids to band together and give joint gifts for shower and wedding—or clearly express that they aren't required to bring shower gifts.

BETTIEQUETTE:
A thoughtful bride will insist that members of the wedding party not bring gifts to any parties, such as showers.

Rein in your expectations about the time your attendants should invest in your wedding plans. You will call on your bridesmaids to listen—endlessly—to details throughout the planning of the wedding and to be available for special tasks such as addressing envelopes, making centerpieces, perhaps decorating the wedding site, attending the showers, rehearsal and rehearsal dinner, and (finally!)

preceding you down the aisle on the big day. Be realistic and sensitive when making demands on their time.

View the maid of honor as leader of the group. This is an important role, so it's important to choose your maid of honor wisely. She will be responsible for organizing the bridesmaids for dress fittings, planning the shower, and anything else that the bride needs during the planning process. On the wedding day, she will take charge of the groom's ring, immediately precede the bride down the aisle, and then sign the marriage certificate as a witness. She'll also be expected to give a charming and thoughtful toast at the reception.

Expect that the bridesmaids will plan the bridal shower. The attendants plan a bridal or couple's shower. The maid of honor will see to the broad strokes, but the bridesmaids will be asked to contribute their time, talent and money in planning a special event.

Expect that attendants will be host-assistants at the wedding reception. If you have a reception line, your bridal party will be part of it. When the reception is in full swing, they will be expected to circulate, welcoming guests, introducing people who are standing alone and ensuring that everyone is well looked after and comfortable.

Here Come the Men: The Groomsmen

The best man is the groom's aide. He organizes a bachelor party for the groom, perhaps working with the maid of honor in organizing a couple's party; coordinating the tuxedo fitting, pickup and return with the other groomsmen; attending the rehearsal and rehearsal dinner; and reminding the other male attendants of the what, where and when of all these events.

Make sure the best man sticks like glue to the groom on the wedding day. The best man picks up the groom and delivers him to the site of the wedding. He has the ring tucked away in an easy-to-access pocket (unless a ring bearer is entrusted with the real ring). He has the envelope with the gratuity for the officiant, which he delivers as soon as the ceremony is over. He signs the wedding certificate as a witness and he gives the first toast at the reception.

Here Come the Children: The Scene Stealers

Choose either girls or boys as flower children. These little ones, aged four to eight, traditionally scattered rose petals, but more and more wedding sites frown on this mess. Today it is more usual for children to carry baskets of flowers or teddy bears or dolls. After they reach the altar, they should join their parents in a pew; it is asking too much to have them stand at the altar throughout the service.

BETTIEQUETTE:
Children in the wedding party add charm, unpredictability and often humor, but be prepared: they also get all the attention.

Ring bearers have traditionally been little boys, but these days, forward-thinking bridal couples are choosing young girls to fill this role.

Consider fake rings for the ring bearers. Traditionally a young boy (but these days sometimes a girl) carries the two wedding rings down the aisle attached to a small fancy pillow. It is wise to use fake rings for this purpose, with the maid of honor and best man in charge of the real rings.

Invent roles for teenagers. You may have young siblings or nieces and nephews who would enjoy being part of the ceremony. Consider having them lead the processional and then light a cluster of candles at the altar.

The Parents

Both bride's and groom's parents (and especially your mothers) have likely been waiting for your wedding day since you were young, so find special ways to honor them.

If you host your own wedding, include both sets of parents so they don't feel left out. It's your wedding and your party and you're doing it your way, but stay in touch with both sets of parents as your plans progress. Inviting them to appointments, using them as sounding boards, asking your mother to do some research for you, and even getting your father to arrange wedding day transportation are ways to make them feel part of your planning.

Invite your father to escort you down the aisle. This is no longer a given in modern weddings. Older brides often prefer not to be escorted. In some religions, both parents escort the bride. And sometimes the bride and groom approach the altar together. If you do extend the honor to your father, you are giving him a gift and memory he will treasure.

Give parents first-row seating. Parents should be given preferential seating even if they are not hosting the wedding. If parents are divorced but neither are remarried, often they will agree to share the first pew. If one or both have remarried, mom takes the first pew and dad takes the second or third pew. The groom's parents are seated across the aisle, opposite the bride's parents.

Invite parents to light unity candles during the ceremony. Involving both sets of parents in candle lighting emphasizes their equal importance to the bridal couple and the importance of the extended family.

Honor parents at the reception. During toasts at the reception, you and your groom should each take the opportunity to tell your parents how they've shaped your lives.

Be sensitive to the mother-of-the-groom. Your soon-to-be mother-in-law's involvement in the wedding planning can elicit reactions ranging from her feeling ignored, to your feeling she's being intrusive. This is a sensitive time when the relationship between you and your mother-in-law can go sour. Be considerate and make gestures that involve all parents, especially the mothers.

Make sure divorced parents' "dates" don't miss out on all the fun. When the solemn nuptials are over, it is time to party. This is Act Two. Parents' "dates" can join everyone at the reception where dad and mom each host their own table. If both the groom and bride's parents are divorced, there can be four parent tables. Why not?

The Extended Family

Pay a special tribute to grandparents. It is surprising how often grandparents get lost in the crowd. See that grandmothers have corsages and grandfathers have boutonnieres. Ensure that they are seated in the second row at the service (or the third row if divorced parents have claimed the first two pews). Most important, see that someone is responsible for getting your grandparents to the site of the photography session so they aren't left out of the formal family pictures.

BETTIEQUETTE:
Acknowledge your
grandparents in your toasts.

Remember stepparents and stepsiblings. Blended families will have preferred seating at both the ceremony and the reception and can be acknowledged at the beginning of the toast that honors the parents and grandparents.

If they can't be part of the wedding party, acknowledge close relatives and friends by giving them special duties. Here are a few examples:

- Invite them to give readings during the ceremony.
- Ask them to meet and greet guests at the door before the ceremony.
- Have them present ceremony programs as guests are being seated.
- Give the women corsages and the men boutonnieres to signify that they are someone special.
- Give these guests priority seating at both the ceremony and the reception.

List everyone who is important to you before you extend invitations to relatives and friends. Recognize that there are limited opportunities to participate in any wedding. It is too easy to become sentimental and impulsive and invite too many family members and friends to play a role. Take your time. Make rational and well-thought-out decisions as to who will do what.

Wedding Party Roundup

Avoid impulsive decisions; take time in choosing attendants.

~

Accept wedding party refusals graciously.

~

Review what is expected of those in the bridal party.

~

Understand the pluses and minuses of including children.

~

Consider ways to acknowledge and include your parents.

~

Honor all those who are close or special to you.

~

Review the options for being escorted down the aisle.

The guest list is a sensitive area, so tread carefully. It's almost impossible to avoid hurt feelings as you build your ideal list and then have to eliminate names.

Seven

The Guest List

Navigate these challenging waters with grace

O ver the months of sorting out details, you will find a whole new meaning to the word *compromise*—especially when it comes to the guest list. Nevertheless, when the date is set and the service and celebration sites chosen, it's time to get to work on the guest lists.

Allocate the number of guests for each of those who are hosting or co-hosting the wedding. This often includes the bridal couple, the bride's parents and the groom's parents. In this instance, allocate one third of the total number of guests to each group.

The allocation can be negotiable based on individual circumstances. You may, for example, be married in the city where you work and your parents may live in a distant town and therefore have fewer guests who will be able to attend.

BETTIEQUETTE:

Nobody can make guest list decisions for you. The best advice is to make a list of possibilities and start eliminating. Be ruthless.

What matters is that everybody involved must be absolutely clear about the parameters, and that no later additions to the guest list are allowed.

Be prepared for one aggressive person to keep adding to their list. Some people have a harder time than others limiting their guest list. One way to get a handle on this is to agree ahead of time that every addition must be accompanied by a deletion from that person's original list. Spell this out early in the game and there will be fewer problems as the planning proceeds.

Beware the manipulative co-host (and it could be you). An insistent person may say, "But I'll pay for my additions." That's never going to happen. Regardless, it sets up an imbalance in the carefully apportioned list. If the person in charge of the list caves in to one aggressive co-host, it can result in hard feelings among the others.

Build your list and then cut it down. It becomes a numbers game. Once the size of the wedding is established, you know your limit. Now list the must-haves: the wedding party, close relatives and close friends. Then start moving the needle. Are neighbors more important than the people you work with? Is it necessary to invite distant cousins you rarely see? Are childhood friends that you sometimes get in touch with important?

Never invite guests to the ceremony and not to the reception. This is the ultimate insult. The reverse, however, is acceptable. It is not uncommon for a couple to want an intimate exchange of vows followed by a large reception. If you want someone at your ceremony, however, you must invite them to the reception.

BETTIEQUETTE:

If you invite someone to your ceremony, they must be invited to your reception.

Have an adults-only wedding. You can choose (and many do) to have an adults-only wedding. In fact it is acceptable to include the words "Adults-only reception to follow" on the invitation. And don't worry: If you have a flower girl or ring bearer in your wedding party, this does *not* open the door to guests bringing their children.

You must be firm. If guests say they cannot attend without their children, inform them that you cannot make an exception—and that you'll miss them!

Beware the manipulative guest. You must be firm with friends who want to add to your guest list. Some assume that they can bring the person they are currently dating, but unless you have explicitly invited them, this is not the case.

Decide whether to invite your boss and co-workers. If you have developed a close personal friendship with one of your co-workers, nobody will be offended or surprised when that individual is invited to your wedding but others at work are not. Other than that, don't pick and choose. Invite everybody in your group, or nobody. Sometimes a boss is invited to represent the group; whether you do this will depend on your relationship with him or her.

Apply this criteria to all areas of your life. Whether it's the eight friends you have dinner with once a month or the group you play tennis with, invite all or none.

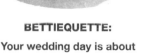

BETTIEQUETTE:
Your wedding day is about tomorrow, not yesterday.

Don't invite past girlfriends or boyfriends. Bad idea! A recent former girlfriend or boyfriend will be a distraction. All eyes will be checking them out, watching their interaction with you and making unwarranted assumptions. If you want to take the attention away from you, this will do it!

Send invitations to any guest eighteen or older. The magic age is eighteen. Every guest of that age or older, regardless of where and with whom they live (and even if they live with their parents), should receive their own invitation.

Invite friends' live-in partners. If a friend is living with someone, that someone should be invited even if you have never met him or her. This is not necessary, however, if your friend is just dating. If you *are* prepared to allow your single friends to bring a date, it's nice to get the names so you can add them to the invitations. If this isn't practical, add "and guest" to the reply card.

Once you decide about dates, don't make exceptions. If you are trying to trim your guest list, it is acceptable to invite single guests to come on their own. Some aggressive singles may add a name to the acceptance card, but show what you're made of! Call them and tell them that your single friends are not bringing dates and you can't make an exception.

Guest List Roundup

Allocate a number of guests to each host.

~

Be firm with aggressive co-hosts and guests.

~

Be careful when inviting co-workers, childhood friends
and past girlfriends or boyfriends.

~

Remember that an invitation to the service includes an invitation
to the reception.

~

Be prepared to trim your list.

~

Negotiate your guest list to control costs.

Your invitation tells much more than what, where and when. It signals the formality or informality of your wedding.

Eight

Invitations and Stationery

The medium is the message

The first item on your agenda is to decide where the ceremony and reception will be held. When you have confirmed both locations, you are ready to move on.

Agree on how many guests you will have so you can order invitations. The wording and style of the invitations are important, because they signal the style of your wedding.

See that the invitation reflects the formality of the wedding. The invitation does much more than relay information about date, time and place. It tells your guests how to dress. If you are having a formal wedding, don't put together oh-so-cute invitations using your baby pictures! It sends the wrong message and your guests will dress for an oh-so-casual wedding.

Let the guests know what sort of wedding to expect. The invitation should tell guests what kind of event the wedding will be. Will there be a sit-down dinner? If not, your invitation might say, "Cocktails and hors d'oeuvres following the ceremony."

Send save-the-date notices. These notices are optional. They may be sent by mail or email as soon as the date is confirmed—preferably at least three months in advance of the wedding. They are especially helpful to those coming from a distance who need time to make travel plans. They need not be mailed; electronic notices are easy and convenient.

Collect invitations before ordering yours. Look through bridal magazines and visit stationery stores to get a sense of the different styles of invitations available. The range is surprising, from cute to funny to formal. At this early stage in your planning, you may not yet have a clear idea of how formal or informal you want the wedding and reception to be. Make this decision before you order your invitations.

Place your order four to five months before the wedding. Your invitations should be mailed six to eight weeks before the wedding, so put in your order well in advance.

You can order online or through your local stationery store. However, you may prefer to see the options in person, judging for yourself the texture and quality of the paper.

Order the number of invitations according to your guest list plus about 20 extra—including envelopes. After you have done the guest list count, order extra invitations, and about 25 percent more envelopes. They're not over-the-top expensive and you are bound to make mistakes as you hand-write the addresses. Some invitations may be returned because of errors in the address and have to be sent again. As well, you'll need extra invitations for your albums and your parents', and it's a nice gesture to send invitations to the wedding party—it is a keepsake for them too.

BETTIEQUETTE:

Remember that you just need one invitation per couple. (You'd be surprised how many people order on the basis of the total guest list!)

Use a computer program to create homemade invitations for less formal weddings. This is not acceptable for a formal wedding, but software is available that makes this an option for informal weddings. Invitations can range from pretty (perhaps threaded with ribbon or decorated with dried flowers) to witty.

Check the availability of envelopes for homemade invitations. It may take a little shopping around to find a good quality envelope the size you need for a homemade invitation and response card. For this reason, don't get too creative with shape and size until you have checked the availability of envelopes for your masterpieces.

Mail an invitation to yourself to check the cost of postage. The weight, when your package is put together, may be heavier than you think. The extras for formal invitations include tissue paper, inner and outer envelopes, lined envelopes, embossed seals and return cards. You may also include a map, hotel recommendations and information about special events planned for out-of-town guests. Find out sooner rather than later if you're going to need extra postage.

Negotiate with your invitation printer. You may get a break on the price if you order all your stationery needs at once. This could include the invitations, thank-you notes, announcements and perhaps cocktail napkins that carry your name. Ask if there is a package price for the larger order. Printed matchbook covers, once a staple extra, are no longer acceptable because smoking is less tolerated.

Printing Options

There are a number of printing options for your wedding day invitations, ranging from the informal to the elegant, from inexpensive to pricey.

Don't get hustled into making an expensive choice. A common mistake bridal couples make when picking their invitations is paying extra for special effects, like engraving. Even if you are planning a very formal wedding, don't feel pressured to have your invitations engraved, unless price simply doesn't matter. While beautiful and elegant, this is about twice the price of thermography, and the truth is that most people don't know the difference.

Select engraving for ultra-formal weddings. This technique is the costliest printing method. A metal plate stamps the words onto the paper from behind, resulting in raised letters. This is very expensive for small weddings because the cost is in the preparation of the plate. The larger the wedding, the more cost-effective engraving is.

Consider thermography, a less expensive alternative to engraving. Thermography also delivers raised lettering, but puts less of a dent in your budget. It creates raised lettering through a heat-based process that fuses ink and resinous powder.

Choose offset printing for textured paper and homemade invitations. This option can deliver color and is the ideal choice for textured paper (which won't work with raised printing techniques). It also is a good choice for homemade invitations to which you may want to add pictures or dried flowers.

Avoid embossing unless you're prepared to pay the price. Embossing is used to create a large initial or a border in a raised technique. Letterpress involves inking an image and then transferring it onto paper by manually pressing the paper against the image. These are impressive but pricey techniques.

Choose calligraphy to dress up your handwritten invitations. Search the Web to find an experienced calligrapher, preferably in your neighborhood. Or get much the same effect by purchasing calligraphy software.

The Appropriate Wording

The wording of the invitation is important. Among other details the invitation provides, it tells guests who is hosting the wedding.

The use of first names, without titles, is becoming acceptable, but titles should be maintained on formal invitations:

Mr. and Mrs. Robert Hazelton

If the bride's parents host the wedding, the wording may be:

Mr. and Mrs. John Jones
[or John and Mary Jones]

request the honor of your presence

If both sets of parents host the wedding, the wording may be:

Mr. and Mrs. Richard Kim
[or Richard and Helen Kim]

and

Mr. and Mrs. Michael Walsh
[or Michael and Alison Walsh]

request the pleasure of your company
at the marriage of [Optional: their children]

Jane Lee
and
Harvey John

**If a divorced parent hosts the wedding with a new spouse,
the wording may be:**

Mr. and Mrs. Jack Martin

[or Jack and Sylvia Martin]

request the pleasure of your company
at the marriage of Mrs. Martin's daughter
Chantal Carr

**If divorced parents jointly host the wedding,
their names should never be put on the same line.
Only the names of married couples go on the same line:**

Maria Rodriguez
and
Daniel Rodriguez

request the honor of your presence
at the marriage of their daughter

**If couples host their own wedding,
the more formal address of "Mr.," Miss," or Ms." is optional:**

Smita Patel

and

Neil Singh

request the pleasure of your company

[or]

Ms. Anne White and Ms. Ruth Lincoln

cordially invite you to their wedding

If it is a traditional wedding and the bride's parents are paying for and therefore hosting the wedding, the groom's parents do not necessarily appear on the invitation. It is a nice (although optional) gesture, however, to include them after the name of their son, as in "William Beaton, son of Mr. and Mrs. John Beaton [or Mary and John Beaton]."

The names of the groom's parents are not necessarily on the invitation if they are not co-hosts. However, if they are paying their share of the wedding costs, they must be shown on the invitations as co-hosts of the wedding.

An informal wedding can be as casual and innovative as your talent and imagination allow. Go for sentiment or go for humor, whichever suits your personality:

SURPRISE!

Michael Turner and Ted Koefler are finally doing it!
Come join us on Saturday, May 14

[or]

Please join us when we express our love
before those who are closest to our hearts
on Saturday, May 14, at Willmer Hall

For formal invitations, include an inner envelope and a stamped response card. The invitations are put into the inner envelopes, which are not sealed. The inner envelopes name all the invitees at that address, including any children being invited (children's names are not on the outer envelope). The inner envelope does not bear an address. The invitations are inserted so that when the flap is raised, the type faces out.

BETTIEQUETTE: Don't feel overwhelmed—the stationery store will help you figure out what you need.

Guarantee you know the exact number of guests by including a stamped response card. Your caterer needs to know the exact number of guests, and this can save you money because you are, after all, paying the caterer per person. There is a tendency today for savvy bridal couples to rely on their personal websites for responses. They forget that older people may not be computer-literate. Sending a stamped response card will pay off.

Make arrangements for your out-of-town guests. Reserve a block of rooms at a hotel and negotiate a special rate for your guests. Include the hotel booking information and maps with the invitation. Sometimes the ceremony and reception venues can supply a map or you can design one on your computer, clearly labeling names of all access roads.

Plan entertainment for your visiting guests. Add an events list for visitors who may stay in town for a few days. If you're having a weekend wedding, it's thoughtful to pass along information about what's going on in your town during their stay. Include local restaurants, shopping centers and sightseeing activities.

Follow rules of etiquette if the wedding is cancelled after the invitations go out. If you have to cancel the wedding and there is little time, you have to bite the bullet and have someone close to you call guests and notify them. A handwritten note is an alternative. If it was to be a large wedding and there is sufficient time, send a printed notice.

A mailed notice is ideal as it avoids anyone having to give a reason for the cancellation—because, in fact, it's nobody's business. It's more difficult to avoid giving an explanation if you are communicating by phone.

If communication by phone is necessary, delegate the chore to family members rather than making the calls yourself, and be specific about what is to be said. (If the reason is a family calamity, such as a death, of course this may be revealed.)

BETTIEQUETTE:

Only in the case of a death is a reason given for cancellation.

If the problem is a breakdown in the relationship, suggested wording might be "I don't know the specifics and it may be rescheduled, but for now it is cancelled."

The mailed note would come from the hosts:

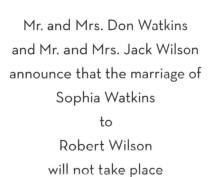

Mr. and Mrs. Don Watkins

and Mr. and Mrs. Jack Wilson

announce that the marriage of

Sophia Watkins

to

Robert Wilson

will not take place

[*Alternative:* has been postponed]

Do not send invitations to those you know will not be able to attend. There will be friends and relatives you care about but who will be unable to attend the wedding. Do not send them an invitation if you know attendance is not possible—this may make them feel obligated to send a gift. Instead send an announcement to these friends and relatives. Mail these the day after the wedding.

BETTIEQUETTE:
The only social event that *requires* a gift is a bridal shower.

Don't make reference in the invitation to your gift registry. This would suggest that you expect a gift. Many people don't know that attendance at a wedding does not require a gift (although we all know that couples certainly look forward to getting them!).

After the wedding, send out name-and-address change cards. This is an ideal way of letting people know whether the bride has kept her maiden name or changed her name, or the couple has hyphenated their names, and if the couple is moving. An alternative way of getting the word out is to order new letterhead or new adhesive labels to put on all your personal mail.

Invitation Roundup

Invitation wording and printing style should signify the formality of the wedding.

~

Order extra envelopes.

~

On the invitation, acknowledge those paying the bills as hosts.

~

Printing techniques vary hugely in cost, so don't be persuaded to make a pricey choice.

~

Consider sending wedding announcements to those who cannot attend.

~

Follow proper etiquette in cancelling a wedding.

Do your homework.
Talk to friends.
Get comparative
prices. It will all add
up to major savings.

Nine

The Negotiations

Sharpen your pencil and cut your costs

Planning a wedding takes a village, and you'll need many different vendors to help you pull it off! Here are the major ones:

- Car/limousine/bus rental and driver
- Caterer
- Ceremony and reception venues
- Clergy (freelance)
- DJ
- Florist
- Makeup artist and hair stylist
- Musicians (service and reception)
- Photographer, videographer
- Rentals (tables, chairs, linens)
- Wedding cake baker
- Wedding planner

Jump on the Web. It's important that the vendors you're dealing with have been aboard the wedding express long enough to fulfill their contracts efficiently and on time. A good way to get a sense of their experience is to check the Internet—search for a good website, check social media and ask for testimonials from previous clients.

Get advice from friends and co-workers. Talk to people you know and trust who have recently been married. They will love to chat about their own wedding and be eager to pass along their advice in every category, from wedding cake to DJ. Be sure to ask about performance as well as costs. Write down their comments for later reference.

Shop around, but not always in person. Comparative shopping may not always require personal visits—this is too time-consuming when you have a full wedding to plan. The Internet is a good starting point for your research. Print out the details, send emails and follow up by phone if you need more information.

Pare down your list and then visit the vendors. You've collected all your data and phoned potential vendors to help you narrow your list to three possibilities for each category. Now, set up appointments.

Appoint either bride or groom to take notes throughout the interview. Ask the vendor to provide a memo of what they are promising and what their costs will be.

Don't forget the details. Get basic prices and then ask for prices on extras that you may or may not want.

Ask vendors to list any surcharges. Avoid surprises when you receive the vendor's bill. For example, if you're ordering a cake, is there a delivery and setup charge? Is tipping for the servers built into the catering cost? Do the photographer and videographer add a surcharge if you want them to hang around for the cake cutting?

BETTIEQUETTE:
The more details you get from the vendors, the better. Receiving estimates doesn't involve making a commitment, and it will give you a benchmark for comparison. You can always go with another vendor.

Flex your bargaining power. Don't be afraid to negotiate. Vendors often seem cool—they know how to play the game and that it's not smart to appear too eager to get your business. You don't want to appear anxious either. Be pleasant, so they know you'll be fair and good to work with, but don't appear too eager. Remember, they want your business, and you have some bargaining power.

Find ways to get a real deal. You're well positioned to get a better deal if your wedding is on a weekday or if your vendor has had a cancellation. If it's a quiet time of year for your vendor, you can also get a reduced rate. But, if he or she doesn't budge as much as you would like in their prices, see what extras they'll throw in for free.

Look for a reason if one vendor's price seems a bargain. Prices can vary wildly among vendors but what appears to be a steal may come back to bite you. Yes, some talented people may offer their services at good prices—perhaps they are just establishing their business, so you are the beneficiary of their introductory prices—but do your research. Why is one price so much lower? Find the answer.

Read your contract carefully before you sign on the dotted line. Every contract, with every vendor, must include every detail about your wedding. Look for the following:

- Your names
- The date and time of your wedding
- The location of the ceremony and reception site
- The specifics of how and if there's a delivery to be made, and the delivery address
- The length of time the person will be on hand the day of the wedding
- A tipping policy
- A refund and cancellation policy
- Detailed contact information for the vendor

BETTIEQUETTE:

If you make any changes to the details, don't do it over the phone—send emails so there's a record. This protects both parties.

Get a receipt when you pay a deposit. When you have chosen a vendor and are ready to make a commitment, be prepared to pay a deposit and ask for a receipt and a copy of the signed agreement.

Ask each vendor when they need to be paid. In most cases, the final payment should be made only after the service is delivered. Here are some guidelines:

- All wedding day attire must be paid in full on pickup.
- A freelance clergy must be paid at the end of the service.
- Service musicians should be paid at the end of the service and reception musicians at the end of the evening.
- Caterers need healthy deposits, usually one on signing a contract, another closer to the wedding and a final check delivered a few days before the wedding, but often post-dated to the wedding date.

Be prepared to make final payment when it's required. Don't be surprised if vendors demand to have the bill for their services paid in full upon delivery—even if that's on your wedding day. Many have been burned in the past by slow-paying customers.

The timing of the final payment is awkward. Vendors need protection because once the wedding is history (the day after the wedding!) hosts may feel less urgency about paying for it. If, on the other hand, you prepay in full and the vendor doesn't deliver, you have little recourse.

It's worth mentioning that vendors will go the distance for clients who are fair and good to work with.

Tipping

The guidelines for tipping wedding service providers are similar to those for tipping in your day-to-day life.

Tip all the lower-paid people who depend on tips for a major part of their income. Many vendors add gratuities to their bill, so inquire about the policy to avoid tipping twice.

Those who should be tipped include the following:

- Delivery people from the florist and baker ($5 to $10 if the delivery is just a dropoff, but more if they are setting up the flowers and cake)
- Limousine driver (15% of the bill)
- The wait staff at the reception (at least $20 each, but be certain that the venue doesn't add the tip to the bill so you don't tip twice)
- Bartenders (10% of the total bar bill)
- Powder room, coat room and parking attendants (50¢ to $1 per guest; do not allow attendants to accept tips from your guests)
- DJ and musicians ($25 for a DJ; $20 for each musician in a group)

Tip your makeup and hair professional as you always do. Some salons offer an envelope that allows you to make a single tip that they distribute to the staff. Others leave it up to you to tip the woman who shampooed your hair and your stylist separately.

BETTIEQUETTE:

If your vendors do an exceptional job, it is a nice gesture to drop them a note after the wedding, which they may pin up in their shop or use in a reference section of their portfolios.

You do not tip the baker, florist, photographer or videographer. These professionals are well paid for their skills. Tip their employees, however, if they are providing a service.

Keep copious notes. Throughout the entire process of comparing prices and then negotiating the best deal, keep notes. Our memories are unreliable and you'll find a notebook that records details invaluable.

Negotiating Roundup

Compare costs and make detailed notes.

~

Shop around, talk to friends, get on the Web.

~

Know who to tip and how much.

~

Negotiate to get no-charge extras.

~

Find out when each vendor requires payment.

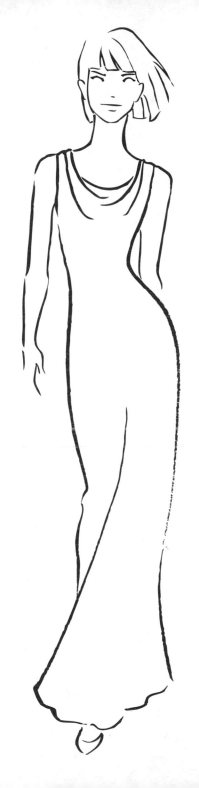

Flowers, candles, trees and fabric set the mood on the big day.

Ten

Flowers and Decor

Set the scene for maximum impact

You want to make your service and your reception memorable It takes only a few fresh ideas to make a difference.

Negotiating with Your Florist

Flowers are the most important, and the most expensive item on your list, and they are central to both the ceremony and reception. On average, they account for about 10 percent of your total wedding budget. It will help if you are working with an experienced florist who knows how to help you cut corners without cutting down on the glamor that only flowers can provide.

Choose flowers in season. Get comparative costs of your favorite flowers, but if budget is a concern, be prepared to accept options.

If you always wanted daisies and they're out of season and would have to be flown in, move on to another choice. Similarly, choose fewer blooms in the bouquets and use interesting "fill" that will substantially cut costs.

BETTIEQUETTE:
Check your financial obligations with your florist if the wedding has to be cancelled.

Get a detailed breakdown of each category in writing. Spell out the exact number of flowers in a bouquet, for instance, so that you can compare apples with apples. This goes for bouquets, boutonnieres, corsages and altar stands for the ceremony. Then get a quote for specific centerpieces, room decor and head-table decor.

Carefully read the contract before signing. The contract must include all the delivery addresses (perhaps bouquet and corsage delivery to your home, altar arrangements and boutonnieres to the site of the service, all room decor to the reception site), your name, date, time and location of the wedding.

Arrange for your florist to have access to the reception hall. In talking to your site manager, be specific about the time the florist needs to decorate the room and be certain that the site will accommodate them. You may have to make special arrangements for someone in management to be on hand to open up or arrange for a key to be supplied.

Flowers and Decor for the Ceremony

Your choice of where and how to display flowers starts with the ceremony site. The service will be solemn, joyful and sentimental—all three and all at once—and adding small touches, such as flowers flanking the altar or attached to pew ends, can emphasize the moment.

Flowers and Decor for the Reception

You can make grand gestures or rely on more subtle and sentimental additions in your decor. Your personal sense of drama will prevail. Some touches require a costly investment, but many can be created at home, perhaps with the help of your bridesmaids. Below are some ideas to make your reception special.

Choose table centers that suit the room. If your reception is in a large room with high ceilings, consider tall, narrow flower arrangements with the interest focused at the top. Not only is this dramatic, but also the height allows guests to chat across the table without the arrangement blocking their view. In a smaller room with lower ceilings, use low centerpieces.

Decorate a forest of small artificial trees. One of the best investments I made for one of my daughters' weddings was to rent thirty artificial trees, all strung with white lights and set throughout the room. All other lighting in the room was turned off, and when the doors were opened, it was magic.

Cluster candles of various heights. Flowers are beautiful, but if your wedding is large, floral centerpieces will absorb a big part of your budget. For an evening event, arrange candles of different heights together and have them lit just before guests arrive.

Edible centerpieces. Place a small wedding cake that serves eight in the center of each table. This will look lovely throughout the dinner and be cut as the dessert.

Set out tasty bites for your guests. Place a small plate with three or four miniature appetizers at each setting before guests are seated. This gives hungry guests something other than rolls to reach for.

Go for "lazy" service. Have lazy Susans in the center of each table. This could house attractive appetizers to tempt guests as soon as they are seated, or a ring of pretty individual desserts to be enjoyed at the end of the meal.

Present pretty fish to be seen, not eaten! Rent fish bowls and buy inexpensive feeder fish. They don't live long but are showy and fun to watch.

Set out bowls of lemons. Fill glass bowls with lemons and then tuck in oversize dried green leaves for a bright, fresh and inexpensive touch.

Provide surprise munchies. Place plates or bowls of munchies or candy in surprising places—just inside the entrance, in the powder room, at the coat check.

Share childhood snaps. Mount childhood pictures of the bride on one half of a large board, and childhood pictures of the groom on the other half.

Release doves for love. Set free a pair of doves at some point during the toasts. This is dramatic and a sure showstopper. Yes, you can rent them. And yes, they are trained to return to the owner.

Go eco with miniature trees. Decorate each table with a miniature tree. They look great, and your guests can take them home after the wedding and plant them.

Create custom cookies. Bake your own cookies and decorate each with the name of a guest. These are edible place cards.

In Jamaica, a dark fruitcake is soaked in rum and sent to friends who are unable to attend the wedding.

Freshen the air. Arrange small, decorative baskets filled with a savory potpourri in the powder rooms. Keep a pretty jar of air freshener available too.

Create your own fortune cookies. Personalize by adding your own fortune to each—romantic quotes from poems are perfect for the occasion. Have a plate of cookies on each table or set one in front of each guest.

Supply washrooms with disaster-saver kits. Have a pretty basket in the washroom with all the items a woman might need to repair any damage: spot remover, hair spray, safety pins, a needle and thread, aspirin, breath mints, hand cream.

Honor thy parents and grandparents. Have a table set up inside the entrance and share wedding pictures of both sets of parents and grandparents. This trip down memory lane will thrill them.

Fill decorative boxes with treats. Buy tiny, pretty boxes in your theme color, fill them with Jordan almonds or other sweets and add them to each place setting. These liven up a table.

Spotlight your menu. Have your full menu printed elegantly on pretty paper and place each on a tiny easel. Use two on a table for eight so there's one within sight of everybody at the table. A menu helps the guests anticipate what is coming—and anticipation elevates the mood.

Wrap table gifts in pretty bags and fabrics. Table gifts like chocolates, soaps, cookies, jars of jam and sweets are perfect in little bags or wrapped in fabric at each guest's seat. Organza, burlap, canvas, foil, velveteen—you'll find a huge variety of options available for order on the Internet.

Repeat your color theme. Your table should continue your theme color. Have rounds of velvet or damask fabric in the theme color placed under gold or silver chargers, for example. A larger round can be placed under the table center.

Get festive. Use as inspiration a major holiday that's celebrated on the month of your wedding. If you are getting married in December, your reception may feature a fully decorated Christmas tree. Create centerpieces from bowls of lovely Christmas tree baubles interspersed with candles. Or set a small evergreen tree in the center of each table, strung with miniature lights powered by batteries.

Add a red rose for love. Red roses are irresistible. Lay a single red rose at the place setting of each woman. This floral touch is especially nice if your table centers do not include flowers (such as clusters of candles).

Ask guests to share their advice. Put a small, beautifully bound loose-leaf book on each table and invite guests to write their advice in it. Later, you can remove the pages and collect them all in one book, a terrific keepsake from your wedding day.

Let guests win a centerpiece. Give guests at each table a chance to win the centerpiece. It may go, for example, to the person with a birthday closest to your wedding date.

Ramp up the music as the evening progresses. Music makes magic. From the ceremony to the cocktail party to the dinner to the dancing, you should give thought to your music choices—they set the mood for the entire day.

Older guests will drift away earlier than the younger crowd. The music can take over the evening as the fun accelerates and the party takes off.

BETTIEQUETTE:

Control the volume of the music. Friends should be able to visit one another during the cocktail and dinner hour without shouting. The music should be subtle during this time.

All the ideas presented here are meant to stimulate your imagination so you can make your wedding day a reflection of your own taste.

Flowers and Decor Roundup

Consider alternative table centrepieces to trim flower costs.

~

Choose flowers that are in season.

~

Make sure your florist has access in advance to the reception site.

~

Have an edible gift at each table setting.

~

Use my decor ideas to jump-start your imagination.

Your lifelong memories of your wedding depend on the talent and imagination of your photographer and videographer.

Eleven

Photography and Videography

Capture these memorable moments

Your wedding day is one that you will want to remember forever—especially after all that planning! Formal and candid pictures can be combined to give you a full and lasting overview of your wedding. These lovely details will slip away if they are not captured. So, do your homework before you commit to your photographer and videographer.

Check out the photographer's style. Instead of viewing just a few shots of many weddings, it's better to see the full range of photos of one wedding. This is the only way to judge the depth and detail of the work. Many photographers these days showcase their portfolios online, on their websites. Do they capture closeups of all the details, from the rings, shoes, bouquets and altar arrangements, to the reception ambience, including guests at each table,

place settings, cake, toasts and first dance? What is the photographer's style: formal and traditional, or informal and candid?

BETTIEQUETTE:

Be clear in your own mind which photography style most interests you, so you choose the right photographer.

Discuss the number of hours committed to your event. Many photographers and videographers leave immediately after the cocktails and before the dinner. To capture the cake cutting, they set up a dummy shot before they leave. If your expectations include them being on hand throughout the event, let them know this, and have the hours built into the contract—but be prepared to pay the piper!

Ensure your photographer and videographer carry a backup camera. Ask if they carry more than one camera. This will be your insurance. You don't want a camera loss or malfunction to cause you to miss photos of this once-in-a-lifetime event.

Request an assistant or second shooter for a large wedding. A photographer may shoot alone, and if the wedding is not too large this is fine. But for bigger events an assistant may be required, and this, of course, will affect the price. A second shooter is not an assistant, but a second professional photographer—and therefore the cost is higher than if you had one working alone. The two photographers don't compete but work out a schedule for each. The photographer and videographer cooperate in much the same way.

If you're on a budget, work with part-time photographers. Your best protection to get the results you want is to work with full-time professionals that specialize in weddings. But if you're counting your pennies, many good amateur photographers and videographers pick up extra money by covering weddings in their spare time.

Give the photographer detailed lists of all the pictures you must have. One list likely will be photos of the bride alone, and with her wedding party and with her family—usually taken before everyone leaves for the ceremony.

The second list will be at the site of the ceremony, with informal shots of the groom and his groomsmen, the arrival of the bride at the site, and the ceremony. If a reception line will immediately follow the ceremony and you want informal shots of your guests, add this to your list.

The third list will be the formal shots of the bride and groom, the group shots of the wedding party and the group family shots during the reception.

Get the name of the specific photographer assigned to you by a large photographic company. Large companies will show a range of work from their various photographers. Be specific about who you want and who will be substituted if that photographer is unable to attend the day of the wedding. Protect yourself against a photographer landing a high-profile wedding and simply sending an alternate or selling off your contract to another photographer.

Specify in writing if you want both black and white *and* color photography. Many young couples want the traditional photography but also want casual shots in photojournalism style, in black and white. Confirm that your photographer is able to deliver both if that is your choice.

Find out what the photographer will provide, and how. These days, most wedding photographers are shooting digitally, which means no film costs. A top photographer can offer well-edited and cropped pictures in albums. An option is to pick the pictures you want and purchase the well-edited digital file. The photographer, however, owns the pictures until you sign the contract, but will likely supply a link to their business website, where you can see the shots from the day, but are unable to print them. Alternatively, there are the more economical photographers who "shoot and burn" everything to a CD. These are exactly as shot, with no cropping or editing.

Discuss what you want with the videographer. Do you want the entire service recorded? Frankly, this is a big yawn for friends and family, and after one viewing you'll find yourself fast-forwarding to get to the meaningful moments. Talk to the videographer about his editing. It should be enough to film a bit of the processional, the exchanging of vows, the sharing of rings and some of the recessional—and, of course, parts of the reception.

Find out how much time the videographer shoots to get a tightly edited result. A half-hour video is plenty long enough, but a videographer needs to shoot as much as two to two-and-a-half hours to get enough material for a well-edited half-hour.

BETTIEQUETTE:

Don't forget your aged aunt or elderly uncle when pictures are being taken. Designate one person to oversee the family photos to make sure that no one is missed.

Don't forget Grandma Jones. It is almost inevitable that when the pictures are delivered, one important relative will be forgotten. Put someone in charge of organizing everyone to get to the site of the after-ceremony photography. Supply that person with a list so the peripheral members of the family aren't left out.

Move the post-wedding pictures along. A pre-dinner cocktail party can drag on because of the delay in completing the bridal party pictures. Guests have to cool their heels while endless pictures are taken. Consider cutting the formal pictures to a minimum, and have a second photographer take informal shots of your guests during the cocktail hour.

Get four prices from the photographer. Two prices are based on the length of time the photographer commits to your wedding, such as the cost of wrapping up before the dinner versus the cost of staying for the full event.

The third and fourth prices are based on how the photos are delivered: the cost of pictures being supplied and you preparing your own albums versus the cost of the photographer preparing and delivering photos mounted in albums, usually one for the bridal couple and one for each of the parents.

Understand seasonal cost variations. The high season for weddings is May to October (with September replacing June as the biggest month of all). Vendors, including photographers and videographers, charge more during this time.

Know that the day of the week affects prices. The heaviest bookings of the week are on Saturday—hardly a surprise. It also shouldn't come as a surprise that many photographers and videographers try to cram in two bookings on those important Saturdays. Be aware of this so you can ask the right questions about their schedules, and be precise about your expectations.

Get a guaranteed delivery time. A high percentage of professionals are in love with their art and their imagination and enjoy the shooting. When it comes time to delivering the results, however, they could take lessons in how to run a small business. It is not unusual for couples to wait six months to get their order. By that time, they may be awaiting the birth of their first child! Lock the photographer and videographer into a time frame, and get everything in writing.

Store your videos and photography to ensure longevity. Store videos upright in their cases and away from electronic equipment that may have magnetic coils at their centers. Store copies of the best of your photos in a fireproof box.

BETTIEQUETTE:

Put a disposable camera on each table as a gentle reminder to guests to participate in capturing memories of your wedding.

Establish a cancellation/refund policy—just in case. When you have stars in your eyes, you can't imagine your wedding being cancelled, but take a reminder from the Boy Scouts: Be prepared.

Get your guests involved. Your friends and guests can provide backup by taking informal pictures with their phones. After the wedding, ask them to share their best pictures.

Photography and Videography Roundup

Check for style and experience as well as price.

~

Arrange for both formal and informal shots.

~

Provide written lists of your must-have shots.

~

Involve your guests in providing pictures.

~

Build a time commitment into the contract.

~

Get prices based on a variety of time and delivery options.

~

Establish a cancellation policy.

Get from here to there by making a time-and-place chart and sharing it with your attendants.

Twelve

Transportation

Traveling to and from the wedding

A ll young girls were once told, "When you go to a dance, you go home with the man who brought you." Well, not so the bride: She goes to the service usually with her father or both parents, but she leaves with her new husband.

The wedding party is similar. The bridesmaids arrive at the service in a group, with transportation arranged by the hosts of the wedding, but they will leave the reception with their spouses or dates. Their arrival can be by bus, limousine, vintage car, horse and carriage, or boat. But they are more likely to leave in private cars. So how do those private cars conveniently arrive at the reception site?

BETTIEQUETTE:
You'll need a spreadsheet to organize the transportation on wedding day. And good luck! It's more complicated than you may think.

Things to Remember
about Wedding Transportation

Book six to eight months in advance. This is critical if your wedding coincides with popular events such as school proms or school graduations, or is on the weekend, when most weddings occur.

BETTIEQUETTE:

When you visit the rental company, take a picture of the car you'll be getting on wedding day.

Start online, but sign on the dotted line in person. These days we seem to do everything online—and that's certainly a good place to start. It's wise, however, to visit the rental company when you're prepared to sign. This gives you the opportunity to see the type of limousine/bus/vintage car you will have. It also ensures that every concern you have is spelled out in the contract.

Understand pricing. There will be a charge for a basic rental—by the hour and likely with a three-hour minimum—and then costs for all the party add-ons that are available.

Use the 30-minute rule. Set the arrival time for the limo or bus about thirty minutes before the actual time you need it. This protects you from stress if there is an unexpected traffic tie-up. If the car does arrive promptly, the driver will be happy to wait for a few minutes while you get yourself organized. Then take your time getting settled and comfortable. This is a day you definitely don't need stress to become your companion.

For how long do you need the limo? It may be hired for the three-hour minimum, or for the entire day and therefore be accessible to the end of the reception. However, count the hours so the cost won't be a surprise. The hourly rate varies across the country but if the cost is $100 an hour (and in some areas, much more) and the wedding day is ten hours (plus a 15 percent tip) the cost of keeping it for the entire day may be a budget breaker.

Have a backup plan. If your mode of transportation includes an engine, there's always the possibility of a breakdown. I recall a bride who wanted to arrive at her wedding a fashionable ten minutes late. When her limousine broke down, she and her parents were stranded because the company had no backup. Everything the company owned was leased. Her ten-minutes-late plans got expanded to an hour-and-ten minutes as they argued with the limousine company and, after a time, just called a taxi.

The moral of the story is to deal with a reliable company that can guarantee a backup in the event of any kind of problem.

Plan for departures after the reception. How will the newlyweds and their wedding party leave the reception? Having a limousine on hand when the reception finally winds down is a pricey option. A good alternative is to have the groom's or bride's own car delivered to the site of the reception the day before the wedding. The bridal couple should drive themselves only if one of them is a non-drinker.

Look after your single wedding party members.
It is the responsibility of the bridal couple to ensure that transportation for the single, dateless bridesmaids and groomsmen is arranged from the wedding site, on to the reception and until they are safely delivered back to their hotels or homes at the end of the evening. The specifics of the transportation should be spelled out to everyone in advance so no one feels they aren't looked after.

BETTIEQUETTE:
No one should be scrambling
to find a taxi at midnight.

Types of Transportation

There are a myriad of types of vehicles to get you, your groom and your wedding party to the ceremony and reception.

Wedding Bus. A bus signals that it's party time! The fun begins as soon as the bus pulls out. Even with a very large bridal party, a bus accommodates everyone, including the bridal couple and their parents. An exception will be the ushers, who should be at the site of the service much earlier than the rest of the bridal party.

Limousines. Next to the family car, this is the most popular method of wedding transportation and limos are available in a wide variety of sizes.

A *luxury sedan* allows the bride to arrive at the site with her father or both parents after everyone else has arrived.

A *ten-passenger limousine* usually accommodates all of the bridesmaids.

A *twenty-passenger limousine* can often accommodate the entire bridal party.

Vintage cars. These aren't easy to find. We hear of car collectors who rent their personal vintage cars for weddings only, but check the Internet. If your area has vintage cars for rent, arriving in a classic that dates back as much as three quarters of a century is sure to impress everyone—especially the men!

Horse and carriage. These are available by the hour with usually a three-hour minimum, or you can get a daily rate that will take you from your house to the wedding site and on to the reception. If you're having a winter wedding, check out the availability of a horse-drawn sleigh.

Boat. If you are being married at a resort, the service may be on the dock or at a nearby chapel. It is exciting if the guests and the groom gather on the dock, waiting for the bride to arrive in a small motorboat. Be certain that all cameras and videos are in action to capture your arrival. Getting out of the boat in a long gown may not be the last word in grace, but it's all part of the charm and an invitation for a few giggles.

Golf carts. If your wedding reception is at a golf club, it makes for great photography and videography if the groom pulls up in a golf cart, followed by his groomsmen, each in his own cart.

Don't drink and drive. A wedding is a great time to leave the cars at home and have taxis ordered. If guests and attendants are in a party-hard mode and everyone will be drinking with no designated drivers, absolutely rely on taxis or book your limos for the extended time. If members of the wedding party have driven themselves to the service and on to the reception and have been drinking over the limit, they should leave the car behind and pick it up the next day. Trust me on this one: a taxi can save a lot of grief.

BETTIEQUETTE:
A wedding is not
the best time to get a DUI.

"Buddy" out-of-town guests with local friends. It's a nice gesture to partner out-of-town guests with local friends so they don't have to order taxis for themselves. Ask your best friends to adopt a couple so that they are picked up at their hotel, taken to the wedding and on to the reception and returned later to the hotel. It's a good idea to have these partners seated at the same table at the reception too.

If this is not possible or practical, arrange taxi service for them and pick up the bill on their behalf. It's not required by etiquette. It's just a thoughtful thing to do.

Before you decorate the limo, make sure it's allowed. Don't assume that the rental company will allow you to add signs or any type of decoration to their vehicles. This is especially true of vintage cars. Have this discussion and then, if it is allowed, ensure it's included in the contract so there is no misunderstanding. If it is not allowed, warn your friends who may be planning to surprise you. The surprise will be the penalty you have to pay!

Arranging transportation may seem a simple task with few options until you start to peel it back, layer by layer—and suddenly it's not so easy. Couples have arrived at their wedding on motorcycles and bicycles-built-for-two. They have jumped out of a plane and been married as they floated back to Earth. They have exchanged vows in the ocean, in deep-sea gear. There seems to be nothing that has not been tried. But those methods of transportation are for a different book!

Transportation Roundup

Develop a chart from arrival at the church to leaving the reception.

~

Get prices on every mode of transportation.

~

Look after out-of-town guests.

~

Use only reliable companies with a good track record.

~

Find out if you're allowed to decorate the car.

Organizing menus is just the beginning. Entertaining your guests well involves the right timing and presentation.

Thirteen

The Menu

Let them eat cake

The menu is an important part of the wedding celebrations. These days, caterers will offer packages that you can change or enlarge—but it's vital to keep track of the costs as you substitute or add to the basic menu.

Before You Begin . . .

If you are having an evening dinner, consider these questions:

- Will you begin with a cocktail hour with servers circulating with canapés and hors d'oeuvres or will you have two food stations so guests can help themselves?
- Will the cocktail hour food options be expansive and expensive? Unusual or familiar?

- What kind of food service do you prefer at the dinner? Table service? Buffet? Food stations? Family style?
- How many courses will you have?
- Will the wedding cake be the dessert? Will there be a midnight dessert table?

Pre-dinner Cocktail Party

The cocktail party is the best time to start the good times and the best place to be adventurous about food choices. Your more sophisticated guests will love experimenting with dishes that may be new to them, even though your more conventional guests may take a pass.

Get creative with the food at the cocktail party. Make a statement. Try sushi; dim sum; sautéed scallops; pâté de foie gras on toast points; authentic ethnic food stations, like Moroccan, Thai or Indian—introduce new and trendy food options, or celebrate your culture in ways that will intrigue your guests.

Don't spoil appetites. Be creative with the cocktail hour menu, but choose only four or five items so guests' appetites will still be ready for the dinner that follows.

Keep the food coming! Have servers constantly circulating with trays so that munchies are available, or present two food stations with your small selection on each so guests can help themselves.

Think variety. Offer options that will satisfy those who enjoy experimenting with new tastes and at least one option that will satisfy conservative appetites.

Provide seating. People expect to stand at a cocktail party, but your older guests may find this difficult. Have at least some grouped seating to accommodate them, and also provide enough room for guests to circulate and chat informally.

Do the math. Take care that you don't run out of food or drink during the cocktail hour. Avoid an embarrassing situation by multiplying the number of guests times the approximate consumption per person.

Assume that each guest will eat about six hors d'oeuvres per hour and allow for three glasses of wine per person. Each bottle of wine can serve five glasses.

Decide how you'll serve drinks. You may want to have an open bar. Alternatively, you can have servers circulating with trays of cocktails, wines and a non-liquor punch.

Serve a signature cocktail. Work with the venue to create a cocktail that's all your own! Perhaps it will match one of your wedding colors, or maybe it will be a flavor that both you and the groom love. You can even give it a special name.

Avoid inappropriate consumption among guests. There are a few ways to control excessive drinking. Pass trays with two shapes of glasses during the cocktail hour so the non-wine and -alcohol drinks are easily distinguishable. One shape may have a fruit punch with no liquor, and the other a signature cocktail.

BETTIEQUETTE:
Don't forget a nonalcoholic version of your signature cocktail for your non-drinking guests!

You may decide to serve only wine throughout the dinner hour with no access to an open bar. The open bar can be reserved for the after-dinner party and dancing.

When it is time to signal an end to the cocktail party and move guests into the dining room, stop food and drink service. If you have had an open bar, shut it down. It's a non-verbal message that will get your guests moving along.

Offer guests a range of foods. There are endless possibilities for the food you'll serve during the cocktail hour, and if you have a caterer, ask for a list of all their options. If you are your own caterer, find a supplier who will work with your menu.

A few options to spur your imagination and your taste buds:

- Mushroom caps stuffed with goat cheese and topped with caviar
- Clams or oyster bar
- Mini grilled cheese sandwiches
- Sushi tray
- Crostini with a variety of toppings—fish, cold meats, cheese, spreads, fruits, olives or toasted nuts
- Cold soup served in shot glasses
- Potato crisps topped with smoked salmon and crème fraîche
- Miniature tomatoes stuffed with avocado and cream cheese
- Platter of international cheeses
- Fruit and cheese skewers

What Kind of Meal Will You Serve?

The time of your wedding will dictate the kind of meal you will offer your guests.

Breakfast or brunch. A morning service can be followed by a sit-down wedding breakfast or brunch with eggs Benedict, grilled tomatoes, potato puffs, fresh fruit, assorted muffins and rolls and champagne or white wine.

English afternoon tea. Almost everybody loves the traditional tea. This is popular if you are planning an early afternoon wedding. Set each table with traditional or Victorian-patterned china. Serve a variety of small sandwiches, warm scones with clotted or Devonshire cream and jam, and one-bite desserts served on three-tiered plates.

Dinner hour. A wedding invariably caters to guests of various cultures and ages, so the dinner entrée should be more conservative than the food served at the cocktail hour.

Limit the number of courses. Keep in mind that people eat less and less and multi-courses are largely unappreciated. For example, you would do well to choose between a soup and a salad; don't offer both. I admit that in some cases, this will depend on the culture, and in this instance, you won't be able to reduce the number of courses!

Be aware of dietary concerns. Some guests may have dietary issues. Low-fat? Vegetarian? Vegan? Gluten-free? You can't cover every option. You might give your guests a choice of two options on the wedding invitation return card so the caterer can be precise in the number required of each entrée.

Be mindful of legal consequences. A wedding reception can be long and, over the hours, involve too much food and too much wine and liquor. Be aware of the possible legal consequences if you serve liquor to minors or allow obviously inebriated guests to drive a car.

Negotiate with Your Caterer

Be prepared to listen to your catere's advice.

Additions to the menu should be in writing and attached to the original contract. You will review the menu after you sign the contract with the site, but almost always there are changes and additions. Protect both yourself and the site by getting every change added to the original quote. (Deal through email rather than the telephone so there is a clear record.) This is important because it avoids anyone playing the blame-game after the wedding.

BETTIEQUETTE:
The best guesstimate for the cost of a sit-down dinner is $120 per person.

The cost per dinner depends on what you'll be serving. It also depends on the site, the quality and selection of the food, how elaborately it's served, and its presentation. Prices also vary across the country. The price of a three-course meal can range from $35 to $135 per person. A casual picnic in the park with sandwiches and salads or a garden barbecue with hot dogs and hamburgers can't compare, in price, to a sit-down dinner in a ballroom. And remember that adding appetizers to a traditional meal hikes up the price.

Ask the caterer if they have a single cost for food and drinks. These days, people consume less wine and liquor than before, and this has given caterers the opportunity to offer a package.

Your Wedding Cake

The cutting of the wedding cake could be the showstopper of your evening. Make it a memorable one.

Choose the style of your wedding before you choose the cake. Is your wedding formal or informal? And beyond that, what is your theme? A medieval wedding, or any wedding with a theme, will dictate the choice of cake.

Understand that today's wedding cake choices are as broad as your imagination. The traditional shape is round, but check out oval, square, rectangle (sometimes with each tier set at a different angle). Think of adding color, perhaps with fresh flower buds.

Think outside the (cake) box. If a tiered wedding cake isn't your style, there are a number of alternatives to choose from. Instead of a single cake, cupcakes are a popular choice. They make a lovely display when stacked on oversize tiered plates. Gourmet doughnuts are a trendy option.

Decide on the icing for your cake. Buttercream icing may be the winner for taste (everybody loves a cake with a buttercream icing), but it is more fragile and needs to be refrigerated. The more practical choice is fondant icing, a rolled dough that delivers a smooth surface wonderful for decorating—and it actually seals the cake and keeps it fresh. Rolled marzipan, an almond paste, also provides a firm surface that envelops the cake and is a good base for decorating.

Ask your baker for a cupcake tester to taste the filling and icing. If this is to be the big dessert at the dinner (instead of a midnight or late-evening coffee-and-cake), the cake-cutting ceremony will happen during the dinner hour and the cake itself needs to taste even better than it looks!

Order extra cake if it is to be the dinner dessert. This extra cake is more than a slab cake. It must have the same filling and icing as the tiered cake. The size of the extra cake will depend on the number of guests. A good baker can tell you exactly what you need and pre-cut the cake for you.

Get creative with your cake topper. There are sophisticated and hilariously funny cake toppers on the market, although some are pricey. Sometimes a talented baker makes the cake topper. Decorating the top and around the perimeter with fresh flowers is less expensive than having the baker make an adornment by hand.

The tradition of a couple feeding each other cake dates back centuries. It symbolizes the couple's commitment to provide for each other. However, the message gets lost when couples smash food in each other's faces! It's hardly a surprise that this custom is losing favor (although guests may think it's hilarious). If you want to play, have your makeup at hand to repair the damage.

Give the cake a spotlight. Of all the food served at your reception, your cake will be the center-piece. Often it is a work of art, so display it at its own table.

Don't forget the cake cutting. The cutting of your wedding cake is a nice moment that should be captured. If your photographer has wrapped up, be sure to have a friend take that picture!

For fun, add a groom's cake to the festivities. The tradition of the groom's cake began in the American southern states, and it is a gift from the bride to the groom. Unlike the wedding cake, it is often a chocolate or liquor-soaked cake with a dark icing and the way it's decorated is a nod to the groom's hobbies and interests. It's a nice idea for the bride to present it to her groom at the rehearsal dinner, where it becomes the dessert. Alternatively, it can be displayed next to the major wedding cake at the reception.

Sometimes a groom's cake is displayed separately and then cut and put into boxes for guests to take home. Legend has it that if single women sleep with a slice under their pillow, they'll dream of their future husband.

Check the reception site's regulations regarding cake. Before you place your order, check the reception site for any stipulations. Some sites insist on their in-house staff providing the cake, some require you to use a specific baker, and some charge a pricey cutting fee if you use your own baker.

Menu Roundup

Be creative with the cocktail party menu.

~

Provide seating during the cocktail hour.

~

Offer your guests menu options.

~

Get additions to the catering menu in writing.

~

Get specific prices for food and drink.

~

Consider an alternative to the wedding cake.

~

Add original touches to make the event memorable.

There's a major shift in customs and practices as couples today choose partners with different backgrounds and experiences.

Fourteen

Marriage Mixes

The changing face of commitment

T wo generations ago, couples who married tended to share the same ethnic and religious backgrounds. The typical bride was in her early twenties, met her fiancé at church or through friends and lived with her parents, and her mother was her partner in planning the wedding. After all, her mother often didn't have her own career and she had been waiting for this moment since her six-year-old daughter was clumping around in her high-heeled shoes and pretending to get married. And, oh yes . . . Daddy paid for everything.

Every one of those earlier certainties has been challenged. Today not only do we have same-sex marriages, but also ethnic backgrounds are more often mixed. Couples often have different religions or don't actively take part in any religion. Mother's influence in the planning of the wedding is almost irrelevant. (She has been replaced by the groom, who is often deeply involved in the planning.) And more than half of today's bridal couples are already living together and almost half host their own wedding.

Some of these changes are due to the current age of couples being married. Today, the average age of the first-time bride is creeping up to thirty. She is established in her career and in her relationship and she and her fiancé sometimes feel that it is inappropriate to expect their parents to finance their wedding. And anyway, if the bridal couple pays their own bills they get to make all the decisions, so the wedding can, in every detail, be exactly what they want. That's a win-win for both the couple and their parents!

This massive change in the wedding landscape affects every aspect of today's weddings.

Invitations

There's a plethora of options available these days, tailored to all different unions.

BETTIEQUETTE:
Some families go so far as to have each family send out their own invitations in their own language, but I don't recommend this. It emphasizes the difference. When both languages are honored in one invitation, it suggests harmony.

Same-sex invitations. Major invitation companies now produce styles that specifically target the same-sex wedding. These often include a picture of the couple, just in case Great-Aunt Miranda didn't get the memo! Some emphasize the same-sex status of the couple with *Mr. & Mr.* or *Mrs. & Mrs.* in large fancy script. The invitations are specifically designed to celebrate the gender of the union.

Intercultural invitations. These invitations can cause family wars, but if two languages are involved, the best solution is to print the invitation in both languages.

Interfaith invitations. If their individual religions are equally important to the bridal couple, and each will stay active in that religion, it is ideal if both religions are represented at the service. This is not always possible, but it is a gift to a couple if they can find accommodating clergy.

This dual representation need not alter the invitation, but if the couple feels strongly about signaling to their guests that both religions will participate, this can be done:

at

St. Joseph Catholic Church
with a blessing by
Reverend Michael Mason

Planning the Wedding

There may be some obstacles to stick-handle en route to the altar when there are major differences in background and expectations. A wedding in a church isn't always possible for interfaith and same-sex marriages, and if you are considering a destination wedding, not all countries are welcoming.

Same-sex weddings. A wedding celebrated other than in a church is still the usual choice. Often it takes place in a private home, but there are lots of options if it is a larger wedding, such as a banquet hall, golf club, hotel, historic house and more. The service itself is often a civil service, although increasingly the officiant is a minister, rabbi or priest who accepts same-sex marriage.

BETTIEQUETTE:

If you are planning a destination wedding, check with the country of your choice. A church wedding is not always possible, but some governments provide civil unions available to gays and lesbians.

Religious institutions are currently analyzing their positions. Today, some rabbis officiate at same-sex weddings, with the wording somewhat adjusted ("bridegroom and bride" becomes "loving companions").

Some Protestant churches have authorized the blessing of same-sex unions by introducing a gender-neutral rite for the blessing of their civil marriages. However, currently in the U.S., for example, the Roman Catholic Church, Southern Baptist Church, United Methodist Church and the Church of Jesus Christ of Latter-day Saints do not perform same-sex marriages, even if such marriage is legal in that state.

Interfaith weddings. With more and more couples of different faiths marrying, churches have policies in place—and they're all different! Protestant religions are so many and so varied that you will need to have a discussion with the minister of your church. The Catholic religion prefers that interfaith couples marry in a Catholic church. If they wish to marry elsewhere, they must get permission from the local bishop. Without this permission, a wedding not held in a Catholic church is not considered valid by the Church. It's usually acceptable, however, for an interfaith couple to invite the non-Catholic religion to be represented at the wedding and offer a few words.

Many rabbis from Reform, Progressive and Liberal Judaism are willing to officiate at interfaith marriages. However, Orthodox and Conservative Judaism do not recognize interfaith marriages.

See if the venue caters to interfaith and same-sex unions. The trend toward bridal couples exploring alternatives to being married in a church has kicked open the door for other venues to develop attractive packages that combine the service and the reception at one site.

Possibilities now include banquet facilities, hotels, golf clubs, museums, art galleries and historic houses. This helps solve the problem of which church wins when the couples don't share a religion. It also is the answer for gays and lesbians whose church may not accept same-sex marriage.

Marriage Mixes Roundup

See that your invitations reflect the union.

~

Check local and religious acceptance of your specific needs.

~

Find clergy who will cooperate.

~

Find out if your venue offers packages specifically for interfaith or same-sex unions.

From engagement party to rehearsal dinner, your life, for a year, will seem to be one long party.

Fifteen

Celebrations

It's all about having a good time

You will never be celebrated more than in the year leading up to your wedding, so stay healthy and fit, and be ready to have fun!

The Engagement Party

An engagement party is not required—it's an option that many couples feel they can do without. And today, most engagements are hardly secret. Everyone knows that the couple is engaged, sometimes within seconds of the proposal, as fast as it can be texted and shared online! But even if the

BETTIEQUETTE:

Couples should be sensitive to their wedding being seen as an excuse to have their hands in their guests' pockets. Don't ask for too much. Don't expect too much. And express your gratitude for the handmade gift or the gift that is given from someone's own home.

Traditionally, the engagement party was hosted by the bride's parents. A formal announcement of the engagement was made, a wedding cake was cut and the celebration ended with toasts.

engagement is not a surprise, a party is a lovely opportunity to celebrate.

Know the options for hosting the party. The parents of the bridal couple, friends or the bridal couple themselves can host the engagement party.

Let your guests know the engagement party is not a gift-giving event. It would be a nice gesture to tell your guests not to bring a gift, and that you just want to share with them the excitement of being engaged. If a few gifts arrive, they should not be opened at the party. Discreetly set them aside and be sensitive to the feelings of guests who didn't bring one.

Recognize exceptions to the no-gift rule. While an engagement party generally is not a gift-giving event, there are exceptions to this rule. If it is part of your culture to give and receive engagement gifts, encourage it to be a sign of affection that doesn't break the bank. A bottle of wine, a cookbook, a book of marriage humor, a gag gift accompanied by a poem or a flowering plant are all thoughtful—and inexpensive—gifts.

Four Guidelines for Wedding Celebrations

Tradition doesn't always fit with our new reality.
But a few rules have not changed,
and should be kept in mind as you plan your big day.

Rule 1. No one should be invited to more than one pre-wedding gift-giving or money-raising event.

Rule 2. The bride should give a gift to the host of a shower and follow up with a handwritten note the next day.

Rule 3. Bridesmaids are invited to all showers, but gifts from them should not be expected. A thoughtful bride will reinforce the message by specifically telling her attendants that they must not bring gifts.

Rule 4. Every gift-giver should receive a handwritten thank-you note and it should be sent as soon as possible after the event. All thank-you notes, for weddings and showers, should be specific about what was received. The only exception is when the gift is money, in which case the sum should not be mentioned. It seems crass to say, "Thanks, Uncle Bill, for the hundred dollars."

Other Parties

While the bridal couple is busy planning a wedding, the wedding party will be planning related festivities, like showers and bachelor and bachelorette parties, to celebrate the upcoming nuptials. Here are some important details.

Wedding Showers

Shower guests and wedding guests. Today there is divided opinion about whether all shower guests must also be invited to the wedding. The standard etiquette has been that they should be. However, customs are changing. People invited to showers may not be on your wedding guest list—like friends of your parents, or co-workers, or casual friends—especially if you're having a small wedding. Wedding showers are a great way to celebrate with everyone in your life, even if you are limiting your wedding guest list.

BETTIEQUETTE:

A shower gift is usually about 20 percent of the cost of a wedding gift. So if guests are spending $200 on a wedding gift, their shower gift should cost no more than $40.

Make things easier for guests with a themed shower. A shower with a theme narrows things down for gift-givers. It may be a kitchen shower where small appliances, cookbooks, linens, or other kitchen accessories are encouraged. (Inviting each guest to include their favorite recipe is a nice touch.) Most brides love lingerie showers, but you may offend old Aunt Hortense if she's horrified by the sexy numbers.

"Plant" a money tree. Not everyone approves of money trees, especially at a wedding, although in some cultures money trees have been used for generations. They lend themselves, however, to a shower because the whole purpose of a shower is to give gifts, and for a bridal couple money is always an appreciated gift. A home-made or artificial tree is set up, and as guests arrive they take a clip and attach their envelope—containing a check or money, and signed with their best wishes.

The Jack and Jill

A Jack and Jill can replace the traditional shower. It is a nice way to include the groom, since the wedding and its festivities can sometimes become all about the bride. The party, which can be themed, just like a shower, is about raising money for the bridal couple. It starts with selling tickets to cover the cost of the venue, music and food. A raffle and door prizes will attract partici- pants and a host of interesting games will raise cash, which is, after all, the purpose of the event. It's safe to over-sell tickets to this party. If a hall accommodates, say, 200 people, sell 250 tickets; typically only about 80 percent of ticketholders will attend.

BETTIEQUETTE:

Thore was a time when grooms were just observers throughout the frantic planning of the wedding. Today's grooms can—and should—be involved from the moment the bride says "I do" to the walk to the altar and beyond.

Find the right venue for the Jack and Jill. This is critical. Research should determine all the costs, maximum occupancy, alcohol policy, liquor license requirement, parking availability and whether the site offers catering and bartending. The hosts may prefer to be in charge of the bar so the profit con- tributes to the bridal fund.

Be fair to the ticket-buyers. While the primary goal is to raise money for the bride and groom, it is important to not short-change the guests. Set a ticket price and see that there is a fair return in fun, surprises and food.

Feed the guests. Hosts might provide a buffet toward the end of the event, or perhaps finger foods throughout the evening. You don't need a large variety of food but you do need a sufficient quantity so that guests don't bail out early because they're hungry. Have liquor and beer available and a range of nonalcoholic drinks. Plan ahead for the liquor license! That's one thing you don't want to forget. Drink prices range from $2.50 to $3.50 each. Jell-O shooters are popular and are usually sold for about a dollar.

Wedding showers are thought to have originated in Netherlands during the eighteenth century. A father didn't want his daughter to marry a poor miller and refused to provide a dowry. The miller, a generous man, was loved by the townsfolk, so they got together and showered the bridal couple with enough goods to build a home. The kind gesture became a tradition!

Get creative with games. Games will be the primary source of revenue. Set up a casino, or games of poker. If you live in a community that doesn't permit gambling and games of chance, you will have to rely on skill-based games, such as darts and golf putting. Include games with a good payoff, because the money raised will be divided between the winner and the bridal couple. You'll find some great ideas on the Internet.

Bachelorette and Bachelor Parties

These are the parties planned by the maid of honor and best man.

Decide on the type of party. The first decision the maid of honor and best man have to make is whether this will be an evening party or a destination party that takes place over a few days. Expense is a major factor. The hosts should take on only what they can afford and what they have the time to organize.

Schedule it well in advance of the wedding. Bachelor and bachelorette parties provide a break from the wedding planning, and an opportunity to have fun, tell rude jokes, probably drink too much, maybe gamble, perhaps get playful with a stripper or two, and often result in a hangover the next day. And that's why I recommend never having this event too close to the wedding. In the past, a blowout on the eve of the wedding too often had disastrous consequences when the groom showed up on his wedding day hungover. Allow recovery time!

The Stag or Bachelor Party

The bachelor party goes back a long way, and over the years has earned a reputation for being raucous and fun. At one time, this party for the husband-to-be involved a black tie dinner hosted by the groom's father. In the more recent past, it involved hazing and humiliation. Today, it has simmered down and is a little more civilized and less about schoolboy antics. This may be because today's grooms are a little older (as are today's brides), having waited to establish their careers before committing to marriage.

In 1890, a stag party thrown by a grandson of P.T. Barnum was raided by police after rumors circulated that a famous belly dancer would be performing nude. Hollywood actor Jimmy Stewart's 1949 bachelor bash at a Beverly Hills restaurant included little people popping out of a serving dish.

Decide on the guest list. Include all of the groomsmen (who will be co-hosts), male co-workers, school friends, any male guests on the bride's and his family's guest list, and relatives, including fathers-of-the-bride and -groom. Have the groom review the list so he can eliminate those he thinks aren't a good fit.

Choose the style of party. The attendants plan the party, but the taste and expectations of the groom should be taken into consideration. Going to a bar and lap-dancing may not be his cup of tea.

Group activity. A game of golf is a popular choice, along with playing baseball or basketball, or paintballing and go-karting. The activity can be followed by dinner and drinks.

Sporting event. The game can be followed by a late-night dinner.

Destination party. The most popular is a weekend in Las Vegas, or a weekend at a tropical all-inclusive resort.

Sport party. This kind of party, perhaps at a campsite or a ski lodge, works well when there are only a few guests.

The bachelorette party is, in many ways, more intimate than the bachelor party. It celebrates a rite of passage and the end of the bride's single life. What began as a few close friends going out for drinks after a shower got kicked up a notch in the 1990s when the bachelorette party became increasingly popular—sometimes involving nightclubs and strippers. Laughter is always center stage! The bachelorette can take many different forms, but all have the same goal: to have fun and share memories and stories.

Decide on the guest list. The average number of guests at a bachelorette party is ten to twelve (although these seem to be expanding). The invitees include the female attendants and closest friends of the bride. Occasionally, we hear of a mammoth party with as many as two hundred guests, but this undermines the intent of the bachelorette party, which should be an intimate gathering to talk about friends' shared past and celebrate the bride's future.

Make this get-together not about gift-giving. The bachelorette does not include gift-giving (other than the bride's expense being covered by the guests), so the bride is often involved in the planning. Sometimes the bride's mother, although not attending, will make a contribution. And sometimes the bride will treat her friends with a special item, such as champagne.

Choose the style of party. Avoid plans that may stretch the pocket-book of even one of the guests. Where you go and what you do is less important than being together.

A weekend getaway. Everyone can gather, say, at a favorite local resort.

Las Vegas. This is a popular destination if everyone can afford it.

A spa evening. Treatments can be followed by a restaurant get-together.

A theatre evening. The show can be followed by a late dinner.

Spread the word. After the plans are set, send out invitations. Emails are fine. This confirms where and when and any other relevant information. Ask for an RSVP. If invited friends don't get back to you, follow up by phone so you know exactly how many will attend.

The Rehearsal Dinner

A North American tradition, the rehearsal dinner is held after the wedding rehearsal. The purpose of the dinner is for the relatives and friends of the bride and groom to meet socially in a relaxed and friendly setting, usually the night before the wedding. If all the attendants are in town, it is best held two nights prior to the wedding, so on the eve of the wedding everyone can relax, organize their clothes for the next day and get a good night's sleep.

Say thank you. At the rehearsal dinner, the couple generally takes the opportunity to thank everyone who has helped with the wedding preparations.

Decide who will host the dinner. The rehearsal dinner was traditionally hosted by the groom's parents—and still will be if the bride's parents are hosting the entire wedding and paying all the other bills. These days, however, wedding costs tend to be shared or are paid by the bridal couple, so the hosting of the rehearsal dinner is up for grabs! Either the bride's or groom's parents may host the event. One set of parents may have it at their home, while the other may offer to bring libations and dessert. Or both sets of parents may co-host the dinner at a restaurant. Many bridal couples host it themselves.

Choose from many venue options. The rehearsal dinner may be held in a restaurant or a private home and may be a table-service dinner or a casual buffet. If weather permits, a barbecue in a garden sets the tone for a relaxed evening. It can be modest and relaxed or a more upscale event—whichever the host prefers.

Include extended family and out-of-town guests. The guests usually include the bridal couple, their parents, the attendants and their partners, friends participating in the service and the clergy, but may also include extended family. It's also thoughtful to invite out-of-town guests who have traveled a great distance to attend your wedding.

Let the venue dictate the menu. An evening gathering in the parents' backyard is perfectly complemented by an informal, unfussy dinner, perhaps buffet- or family-style—whatever affords the hosts the least amount of stress. A self-serve liquor or wine bar is a nice touch. If the site is a yacht club or restaurant, talk to the catering department ahead of time and set a menu for the evening, just as if you were planning a dinner to entertain in your own home.

The Post-Wedding Breakfast

If the bridal couple is still in town the morning after the wedding (and sometimes even if they have left on their honeymoon), parents may host a breakfast or brunch. This would include out-of-town guests, family and close friends. It is a nice gesture and allows everyone to talk about the sentimental and funny things they noticed at the wedding. Some may have cameras loaded with pictures they can share.

All in all, from the engagement to the post-wedding breakfast, weddings are all about parties. Each event will offer something special to remember.

Celebrations Roundup

Be clear about who is hosting, and therefore responsible for every event.

~

Plan ahead and write out every detail for later reference.

~

Time events carefully. If possible, schedule none for just prior to the wedding day.

~

Don't plan anything that will embarrass the bride or groom.

~

Be inclusive so nobody is forgotten.

~

Recognize that not every wedding-related party involves gift-giving.

Be witty,
be sentimental,
but best of all,
be brief.

Sixteen

The Toasts

Find the right words

Toasts elevate your wedding celebration from a party to a reception. They're the component that focuses full attention on the spirit of the day as your guests settle back and prepare to be entertained.

Decide on the order of the toasts. The order varies depending on formality and personal preference, but the toast to the groom is the only mandatory toast and is always first. It is logical that the toast by the maid of honor is next. While this toast is optional, it is increasingly expected.

Here is one popular scenario:

- Best man: toast to the groom
- Maid of honor (best woman): toast to the bride
- Bride's father, mother or both: welcomes the groom to their family

- Groom's father, mother or both: welcomes the bride to their family
- Host(s) of the wedding (and it may be just the bridal couple): acknowledges the guests
- Bridal couple: acknowledge their parents (this is a warm comment, but not a toast)

Keep it short and sweet. Talk to those who are giving toasts and set a time limit. Nobody needs more than two or three minutes to convey their message. Be aware that many people are entranced by the idea of speaking into a microphone and being the center of attention. They need to be reminded that a toast is not about them, but about the person being honored.

Decide on the timing of the toasts. In the past, toasts were the last formal event before the party began. But it's a great idea to have toasts throughout the dinner to keep the focus on the head table. To begin, your MC may give a general welcome and read any special notes received from far-away family and friends who couldn't attend. The first toast can be after the appetizer. And the next, after the dinner. If toasts are delayed to the end of the meal, guests begin to concentrate on their own group and that results in what sometimes seems like a number of separate smaller parties.

Enjoy toasts at an afternoon wedding. At a cocktail party or afternoon tea, the best man's toast would be given as soon as everyone has arrived and likely is followed by the best woman's toast to the bride. The host has the last word.

BETTIEQUETTE:

When something crass or embarrassing is said, the couple shouldn't react and they shouldn't be embarrassed— that is owned by the oaf at the microphone. Accept their poor taste with grace, maintain a neutral face, resist the urge to respond and you will win the admiration of your guests.

Remain seated while you are being toasted. You are seated but everyone else stands to honor you. Never drink a toast to yourself. So whether someone is teasing you or singing your praises, you sit with a smile on your face while everyone else is standing and raising a glass in your honor. At any other occasion, the person being toasted can then stand and respond to a toast. But not at a wedding. The bridal couple stay seated and accept all the toasts without responding.

Allow the host to say a few words. The host was once the father-of-the-bride, who also paid all the bills. But today the parents of the bride are rarely the sole hosts of the wedding. If the groom's parents have ponied up their share of the costs, it is appropriate for both families to take the bows as co-hosts of the wedding and both, in turn, can acknowledge the guests. The hosts' remarks follow the toasts.

Thank your family and guests. When the bridal couple hosts their own wedding they thank their guests for sharing their day. This includes thanking their parents and attendants for everything they've done. No glass is raised. It is simply a heartfelt acknowledgement of those who are close to them.

Do not allow spontaneous toasts. The MC should not hand the microphone to anyone who spontaneously wants to give a toast, drunk or sober. Firmly tell them that the toasts are choreographed and can't be changed.

BETTIEQUETTE:
Keep a firm grip on that microphone to avoid any impromptu toasts and speeches.

Recognize that some people should not give toasts. Don't let anyone who is drunk near a microphone. It is best to cancel a toast rather than have someone with a microphone in hand who is incoherent, rambling and potentially embarrassing.

Be sensitive during your toast. The guests will include a wide variety of ages, all with their own life experience. Both content and language should be sensitive to this and risqué jokes or references to the couple's past in the dating game should be avoided.

Don't tell inside jokes. The best man and best woman have their own history with the couple and there is a temptation to recall their own hilarious incidents. But stories that can't be fully shared with the guests should be avoided. If you hear the words "Mike and Mary know what I mean! *Wink! Wink!*" The audience is lost, and they'll feel left out.

What to Drink and Where

In North America, the traditional drink is champagne. This is a custom but not a requirement. The glass can be raised with any non-alcoholic drink or any wine or liquor. Sometimes the choice is connected to the couple's ethnic background. Non-alcoholic beverages are preferred in Afghanistan, Algeria, Argentina, Egypt, India, Iran, Iraq, Kuwait, Morocco, Qatar and Saudi Arabia, where, in most cases, alcohol consumption is not allowed.

The preferences of other countries:

Australia: beer or rum

Austria: beer

Bahamas: rum

Belgium: beer or wine

Bermuda: rum

Bolivia: rum

Brazil: cachaca

Bulgaria: plum brandy

Canada: rye, beer, champagne

Chile: pisco (a grape liqueur) or wine

China: mao t'ai

Colombia: aguardiente or rum

Costa Rica: guarro

Cuba: rum

Denmark : schnapps

El Salvador: wine

France: champagne

Germany: beer or schnapps

Great Britain: Scotch whisky, beer or wine

Greece: retsina wine or ouzo

Iceland: schnapps

Ireland: Irish whiskey

Israel: wine

Italy: wine

Japan: sake

Mexico: tequila

Netherlands: Dutch gin

New Zealand: beer or wine

Norway: akevitt

Poland: vodka

Portugal: port wine

Russia: vodka

Sweden: akvavit

U.S.: champagne, wine or wedding punch

All of which proves that it's not the libation that counts, but the spirit of the event and the words that are chosen to celebrate the occasion.

Giving a Great Toast

Your wedding party will want to drink to you and your groom. Here are some tips for them to ensure successful toasts.

Play on your strengths. Some people are funny and others are sentimental—just be yourself.

- Introduce yourself and establish your connection with the person you are toasting.
- Don't try to be a Jon Stewart. It's the rare speaker who can tell jokes successfully, so unless you're one of the few, go for sentiment instead of a stand-up routine. It's safer. And you won't embarrass yourself.
- Don't bury your head in your notes, even if you're reading your toast. Keep your head up, making eye contact with your audience.
- Speak clearly, and you may need to slow down (unless your natural speech pattern is slow, in which case speaking even more slowly will drive your audience nuts).
- Don't apologize. It's not about you and your audience doesn't need to know that you're nervous. Keep that piece of unnecessary information to yourself.
- Make it warm and personal, but if you need help, turn to the Internet for famous quotes. Chances are someone has said it better than you can!

Use gentle humor. You will have a personal story or two about the couple, but the best approach is probably to use someone else's words. Don't try to be entirely original—turn to the humor and wisdom of great writers. Ensure, however, that the humor is in good taste and suitable for all age groups.

Here are some samples of humor that won't offend:

"Laugh and the world laughs with you. Snore and you sleep alone."

"Women love us for our defects. If we have enough of them they will forgive us everything, even our intellects." —Oscar Wilde

"This being in love is great—you get a lot of compliments and begin to think you're a great guy." —F. Scott Fitzgerald

"Take each other for better or worse, but not for granted." —Arlene Dahl

"There is nothing nobler or more admirable than when two people who see eye to eye keep house as man and wife, confounding their enemies and delighting their friends." —*The Odyssey*

"Don't overanalyze your marriage: It's like yanking up a fragile indoor plant every twenty minutes to see how its roots are growing." —*The Bill Balance Hip Handbook*

Use quotes effectively. There is no lack of funny and wise quotes. The trick to using them effectively is to find those that, in some way, tie in with the personalities and the relationship of the couple. Then begin and end the quote by spelling out what that connection is.

If, for instance, their relationship started as a friendship, try one of these:

"It is not a lack of love, but a lack of friendship that makes unhappy marriages." You might add: "This comment was said more than a century and a half ago by German philosopher Friedrich Nietzsche, and holds true today. Mike and Mary are a perfect example because, as we all know, their relationship began with a great friendship and grew from there."

"Meeting you was fate, becoming your friend was a choice, but falling in love with you was beyond my control." The author is unknown but his thought resonates on this special day because nobody knows the truth of this better than Mike and Mary.

If the couple has a sense of humor, give them advice: This might be prefaced with, "I have a little advice to pass along . . ."

"To keep your marriage brimming,
With love in the loving cup,
Whenever you're wrong, admit it;
Whenever you're right, shut up.
With a bow to Ogden Nash because that's good advice for all of us. How many here have learned this one the hard way? Take note, Mike and Mary."

"Winston Churchill, obviously sentimental, said 'My most brilliant achievement was my ability to be able to persuade my wife to marry me.' I think that this is Mike's greatest achievement, too."

"People have been having their say about marriage for a few thousand years. It was Socrates, born in 470 BCE, who said, 'My advice to you is to get married. If you find a good wife, you'll be happy. If not, you'll become a philosopher.' We all know that Mike has found his good wife and Mary has found her good husband."

"One of the wisest quotes I've heard about marriage is this: 'A successful marriage requires falling in love many times, always with the same person.' Nobody seems to know who originally said this, but what we do know is how true it is. I wish Mike and Mary a lifetime of falling in love over and over again."

Keep notes handy. Write the toast out in short form, in large type, with key words underlined or in color.

Don't brag about being unprepared. A toast should never be started by saying "I haven't prepared anything so I hope you'll bear with me." This is too often used to get the sympathy of the audience, but the result is quite the reverse. It is insulting that the speaker's time was too valuable to waste on something as unimportant as this wedding.

And never wing it. Sometimes a person is comfortable in front of an audience and is certain they can improvise. They may be accustomed to being in front of co-workers or be confident within their own professional environment, but this is a totally different experience. Winging it never works. Prepare. Write it out. Have notes at hand.

Relax, Nervous Nelly. If the speaker is nervous, the audience will be edgy too. It is far, far better to read a toast, occasionally pausing and looking up at the audience, than to rely on your memory and get yourself (and your audience) in a state.

It's not about you. Some speakers talk exclusively about their own relationship with the bride or groom and the toast becomes all about them. Check the ego.

Should you be funny or sentimental? Both are great. But don't use humor that will embarrass the couple. No anecdotes about their dating history, please.

Other Occasions for Wedding Toasts

The engagement party. Whoever is hosting the party should offer a toast midway through the event. If one set of parents has thrown the celebration, they should greet the guests and formally announce their pleasure about the upcoming nuptials, and then acknowledge the engagement—including welcoming the new son- or daughter-in-law to the family. The bridal couple should respond with their thanks and gratitude. The other parents then have the option to give a similar toast.

BETTIEQUETTE:

When it comes to giving toasts, brevity is gold.

The rehearsal dinner. Whoever hosts the dinner gives the first toast. These days, the dinner is often hosted by the bridal couple themselves—especially if they are hosting the entire wedding. Because it is a casual event, it can be followed by spontaneous—and longer—toasts from the best man, the best woman and even good old Aunt Bessie.

The bridal shower. The host of the shower welcomes the guests, says a few words about her connection to the bride and closes by congratulating the couple and inviting everyone to have a good time. This is a welcome, but not a toast. You should respond by thanking your host. At the end of the shower, repeat your thank you to your host and thank everyone for attending. This will include a general thank you for all the gifts, acknowledgement of the bridesmaids for all their help and, especially, a few words about your mother and other close relatives, such as grandmothers, godmother, sisters and aunts.

Wedding toasts are all about recognizing both the event and the people involved. They make a significant contribution, so be sure to have a videographer on hand to record them. The excitement may, at the time, obscure your drinking it all in. Many couples tell me that they enjoyed the toasts even more when they viewed them long after their wedding day.

Toasts Roundup

Choose those who will be giving toasts with care.

~

Be prepared. Write it out. Rehearse.

~

Avoid inappropriate or embarrassing remarks.

~

Decide who toasts whom—and when.

~

Know the etiquette of toasting.

~

Get help from famous people.

You will receive more gifts for your wedding than you ever will again. But there's more than getting. There's giving.

Seventeen

The Gifts

Your special day is about more than getting

W hat could you possibly need to know about getting or giving a gift? There is a special occasion, a gift is presented and the recipient says thank you. So easy! Well, hold on. As it happens there is a graceful art in getting, and a few potholes along the road to giving.

Of course you will look forward to the wedding and shower gifts you will receive, but you will be giving gifts yourself to attendants and friends who help you throughout the months of planning.

The getting is hugely exciting, though, so let's start there.

Getting Gifts

It's a good start if you understand the traditions and etiquette around receiving gifts because bridal couples sometimes have unrealistic expectations. Frankly, it's not unusual for greed to raise its ugly head! So remember that there's more than just *getting*; there's getting with warmth and a timely response of thanks.

Adjust your expectations. Bridal couples sometimes forget that a guest's acceptance of your invitation to the wedding does not *require* them to send a gift. Think of your wedding as you would a dinner party at your home. A dinner guest is not required to bring a hostess gift, but most do. Similarly, it is rare for an individual to attend a wedding and not send a gift. However, if Aunt Sally lives alone and exists on a small income, it would be a nice gesture to say, "Please don't bring a gift. I just want you with me on my wedding day."

The only social events that *require* either gifts or money are a bridal shower and a Jack and Jill, because the purpose of these events is to "shower" the couple with money or gifts.

The Gift Registry

Have one registry at a department store with branches across the country so guests from sea to sea can access your list. Major stores will help you set up your registry online so everything from choosing gifts to arranging delivery and even gift-wrapping can all be handled digitally. Guests visit your page, see the entire list (along with prices), make their choice and pay with a credit card. That item is then removed from the list to avoid duplication. You also can add to the list at any time. This makes it easy for your guests— they can do it all from the comfort of their own living room.

If you belong to a culture that traditionally gives money, you are still wise to open a gift registry because some guests prefer to give a gift and a registry protects you from receiving items you don't need or want.

Open two or three gift registries to ensure you receive what you want. Your second or third registries hone in on specific categories of gifts, such as a china store that carries the specific lines and patterns that you want. Or one may be a sporting goods or hobby store, or any other specialty store that reflects your interests.

Set a registry up before gift-giving events are scheduled. How soon you set up the registry depends on how soon the wedding follows the engagement. Be certain that your registry is in place and available to guests before shower-planning begins.

Include every price range. Shower gifts are less expensive than wedding gifts, so include items in your registry in a wide price range to accommodate both events. The best registries mix high and low prices and a variety of items so your guests will have no trouble finding something that suits them.

BETTIEQUETTE:

An invitation to a wedding should have no connection to the expectation of receiving a gift.

Do not enclose any reference to a gift registry with your wedding invitation. Registry information must never accompany a wedding invitation; that would confirm that a gift is the price of admission!

Know that not all guests will use the gift registry. Some guests won't use the registry—they may prefer to make their own choice. This is their decision—and don't commit the faux pas of one bride who actually returned a gift to the giver, insisting that they choose one from her registry.

Regardless of the gift's genesis, receive it with a smile and respond with a warm thank-you note.

Traditional Gift-Giving

Every wedding is a union of two families—not just a union of a couple—so you (and your guests) may want to inform yourself about the bridal couple's cultural traditions.

- Many southern Europeans receive cash for the wedding gift. The usual amount is to cover the approximate cost of your dinner plus a little extra.
- Northern Europeans, and especially the English, traditionally give gifts.
- Guests at a Chinese wedding give money in a red envelope—enough to cover their dinner. The closer the relationship, the more money is expected. Don't give a clock, towels, umbrella, sharp objects such as knives and scissors or gifts in sets of four as all of these signal bad luck.
- Japanese guests also give money, presented in a decorative envelope. The amount should be an odd number; this is symbolic, so it can't be divided by two. The bills must be new and can be ordered through the bank (although today most guests will just enclose a check in the envelope).
- Jewish wedding guests often give gifts of money. When giving a monetary gift, it is considerate to give in multiples of 18. *Chai* is the Hebrew word for *living* and it also represents the number 18. Rather than giving $100, give $108 ($6 x $18).
- An Indian couple would be pleased with household items, but a traditional Indian wedding gift also could be gold and silver jewelry. Don't wrap gifts in white or black. These colors are bad luck. When giving money, give an odd number—for example, $101 instead of $100.
- Hindus should not be given gifts made of leather. Muslims should not be given gifts made of pigskin or any alcohol products.

In North America, most of us import the customs of our ancestry. So, let's assume that your background is English and you are invited to an Italian wedding. Should you give cash or a gift? The decision belongs to the giver, not the receiver, so do whichever you please. Guests are not obligated to follow the ethnic customs of the bridal couple.

Saying Thank You

A verbal thank you *never* replaces the written thank-you note, regardless of its warmth and sincerity.

Be timely in your thanks. Someone, sometime, started a myth that bridal couples have a year to send out their thank-you notes. Not true! It really is insulting to be thanked for a gift months after it is given. This myth has been enthusiastically embraced by some couples; it has become a convenient excuse for procrastination. But it shows a lack of appreciation for all those great gifts.

BETTIEQUETTE:
All thank-you notes should be sent within one month of the wedding.

Send a handwritten thank you in a hand-addressed envelope. A general printed thank you, regardless of how attractive it is, is totally unacceptable. So are computer-generated address labels. So is sending thank-you notes via email. Show the gift-giver that you cared enough to put a little effort into your response. Choose attractive notepaper that reflects your style so you can appropriately express your appreciation in a handwritten note.

Be thoughtful in your thanks. Your note can be short but it should always mention the specific gift and how you will use or enjoy it, even if that's stretching the truth just a little! There is only one exception: When you are acknowledging a gift of money, the amount should not be mentioned.

Write your thank-you notes—for both shower and wedding gifts—as they are received. If you stay on top of writing your thank-you notes, and make a goal to respond as soon as you receive the gift, the task doesn't build and become overwhelming. Keep a detailed record of every event, the date of the event, the details of every gift and the date of your response.

If you're given a gift from a large group, a group thank you is appropriate. If a large group (such as your co-workers) gives you a gift, it is acceptable to write a note to the group that can be posted up or otherwise circulated at your place of employment. If a small group, such as your attendants, gives a joint gift, each person must receive a personal note from you.

Acknowledge co-gift-givers in your thank-you notes. When you are writing to co-gift-givers separately, refer to each in the body of each note. This indicates that although each note is addressed to only one of them, you are acknowledging both. For instance: "Dear Ann, I want to thank you and Stacie for the great wok. You are both so thoughtful! Mike and I love to cook, so you can imagine how often we will use it." And then, "Dear Stacie, you and Anne couldn't have given us a more thoughtful gift. Every time we use the wok, we will think of you."

Easily build an address list at your bridal shower. The current trend of handing out envelopes at a shower for each person to address for the bride with their own addresses is an unfortunate one. A better alternative is to pass around a book and have everyone enter their name and address as a memento of who attended. Bingo! You also have captured their addresses.

Have the groom do his share. Writing thank-you notes was once the bride's responsibility, but now it is shared. The groom might take on the task of writing to his parents' friends while the bride tackles the notes to her parents' friends. The rest of the list can be shared. Remember that it's charming for both bride and groom to sign all the notes.

Problem Gifts

For your showers and wedding you will receive more gifts than you will ever receive again, and you hope to receive the things you need and want. But because the choice of gift rests with the givers, that won't always be the case. Be prepared to be enthusiastic about every gift—however much you don't like it!

Grin and bear it. A gift must never be returned because it is not to your taste or doesn't meet your needs. (Yes. Brides have been known to return a gift and ask the giver to use her gift registry. But that's inappropriate.) Remind yourself that the spirit of the gift is more important than the gift itself.

If a gift receipt is included, clearly the giver doesn't mind if you return or exchange the gift—in fact, they're signaling it!

Treasure the thoughtfulness. Sometimes an older relative passes along something from their own home, hoping that you will cherish it. Regardless of your opinion about the gift, accept it warmly and, in your thank-you note, reinforce their sentimental thoughtfulness and your delight in having something from their home.

Be discreet about duplicated and damaged gifts. If a gift is duplicated, the gift-giver should not be told. Quietly make an exchange. If a gift is damaged and it came from your registry, get in touch with the store to have it replaced and don't tell the giver. Only if it did not come from your registry will you tell the giver, who likely has a receipt and can address the problem. If the gift is obviously not new (and likely comes from the giver's own home), mum's the word.

Asking for Cash

While you may want it, it is inappropriate to ask for cash. Here's why: First of all, there is an assumption that a wedding gift is expected. Second, the giver always chooses the gift.

Be aware that cash showers have become acceptable. This is because (a) the purpose of a shower is to give gifts to the couple and (b) the host of the shower is someone outside the family. Friends sometimes host tree showers, in which checks in envelopes are pinned to a shower tree.

Don't open envelopes with cash at a shower or wedding. The amount never should be revealed in front of other guests. The thank-you note will refer to "the generous gift" and might go on to suggest how the money will be spent.

If you're hosting a shower-tree event, don't set a contribution amount. This is the choice of the giver. It is not unusual for a guest to call and ask if the host has any idea how much others are giving, and if she knows, she might say, "Oh, I gather that several guests are giving $25, but it's entirely up to you. The envelopes won't be opened at the shower. The bride will just pick them off the tree and take them home."

Giving Gifts

Over the coming year many people will be involved in your wedding planning. Sometimes brides and grooms get so caught up in their wedding that they assume it is front-and-center with their attendants too. These women and men contribute both their time and their money.

Acknowledge your wedding party with a thoughtful gift. Each should receive a gift, but the gifts need not be identical. Each gift may be something that matches the attendant's interests, reflects your appreciation for their investment of time and money, and acknowledges their contribution to your big day. Usually, a more important gift is given to the best man and best woman.

Gift Ideas for Women

Here are some gift ideas for your bridesmaids:

- Gym bag filled with lotions and shower essentials
- Hobby accessories
- Bookends and a favorite book
- Perfume
- Jewelry, like earrings or a bracelet
- Something monogrammed
- Spa gift certificate
- Desk or decorative clock
- Theater tickets
- Crystal bowl or vase

Here are some gift ideas for your groomsmen:

- Engraved cufflinks
- Case of wine (for connoisseurs)
- Leather or brass clock
- Desk accessories
- Scent
- Sport accessories
- Hobby accessories
- Tickets to a sporting event
- Theater tickets

Make your gift to attendants all about them. You may wish to host a luncheon or dinner for your attendants and then give each their gift—perhaps as they leave, if you want to avoid having them make comparisons about who got what!

Sometimes a bride gives a gift that is really a gift to herself. For instance, she may want her maids to wear their hair a specific way and so she gives them a visit to her hairdresser. Not acceptable! The gift should be tangible and personal and relate to the recipient's taste and interest—something that can be enjoyed long after your wedding day.

Thank the bridal shower and other party hosts appropriately. A thank-you note is not enough! The hosts of these events have invested time, imagination, money and effort into making these events fun and memorable, and each should receive a gift.

These hosts should be acknowledged in three ways. Bring a gift with you so you are sending an immediate message that you appreciate their efforts; thank the host in front of guests at the end of the event; and send a thank-you note the next day. These days, a long email is acceptable, although a snail-mail note on pretty stationery is always appreciated.

Present flowers as a hostess gift—as long as they're in a vase. Don't bring cut flowers to a host or hostess who is giving an event in your honor. They are busy greeting guests and organizing food and don't have time to find a vase and arrange flowers. If you do choose to arrive with flowers, bring a plant or have cut flowers already arranged in a vase.

Thank those who gift their talents. Give a gift to those who contribute to your wedding in a special way. You may have a friend who is an experienced baker and offers to bake your wedding cake. This is a huge gift, and a small token accompanied by a thank-you note will express your gratitude.

Friends may help with everything from providing transportation to making a video to preparing standards of flowers for the service. Other gifts come in the form of hospitality, such as offering room and board to wedding guests. Each should receive a thoughtful gift from the bridal couple.

A talented friend may agree to sing at your wedding. Acknowledge the vocalist in the same way you acknowledge your attendants.

Does the officiant get a gift? If the officiant's service is a gift, have them thanked at the reception if they're attending, and send a note after the wedding. If you are paying for his or her services, enclose the check in a sealed envelope and give it to the best man, who in turn will present it to the officiant just after the service.

Whether you are giving or getting, there are ways to make everyone feel appreciated. Invest a little time in doing both appropriately and your pleasure will be multiplied.

Gifts for Parents

Make a special gesture to your parents. You might, the day after the wedding, send flowers to both families with a warm note as a way of saying thank you for all their support. An alternative would be a phone call from the airport en route to your honeymoon as you wait to board the plane, or when you arrive at your honeymoon destination.

Buy a gift and present it to Mom and Dad before the wedding day. This may be presented at the rehearsal dinner. It may be a gift certificate for a dinner for two at a special restaurant. Obviously, both sets of parents should receive this special attention, especially if both are involved in the wedding planning.

BETTIEQUETTE:

There should be no surprises. If the groom surprises his bride when there was an agreement to skip the gifts, it may backfire. The bridal couple gift exchange is a long-standing custom that may have lost a little of its luster. It's now considered optional.

Whatever your choice, your parents will be thrilled if you acknowledge their lifelong commitment to you as well as their help throughout the planning of the wedding. They will love to be able to say to their friends, "The kids did such a nice thing . . ."

Exchange gifts as bride and groom. In the past, it was the custom for a bridal couple to exchange wedding gifts—often jewelry or an engraved keepsake. Discuss this with each other, because with more than half of today's bridal couples already living together and sharing expenses, they may agree this is one expense they can eliminate.

Gifts Roundup

Weddings are about getting—but also about giving.

~

Gift information must not appear on wedding invitations.

~

Sign up with one national department store.

~

Add another registry or two for specific products of interest.

~

Acknowledge gifts with handwritten notes.

~

Sorry, folks: you can't ask for cash.

~

Make a list of people who should receive a gift from you.

It's all about doing
the things you most
love to do—and
doing them together.

Eighteen

The Honeymoon

Plan your trip of a lifetime

P repare for your honeymoon, just as you did your wedding.

A successful trip depends on you doing your homework. (Preparation: how many times have I talked about that in this book?) It's the best insurance policy against disappointment.

Don't plan the honeymoon in secret! The groom does not fly solo. There's magic at the end of the rainbow but it depends on the planning. That's part of the excitement—and it brings us to suggestion number one. The groom should not plan the honeymoon in secret. It happens more often than you might

BETTIEQUETTE:
The groom thinks planning a secret honeymoon is a romantic gesture, but it's a disastrous beginning. The bride who feels pressured to go along with his great idea will inevitably end up resentful. So honeymoon planning starts with communicating and ends with negotiating.

think: the bride discovers the destination when she gets to the airport. Surprise!

Make planning collaborative. Together, make lists of your favorite things to do. Some travelers like to explore cities, and so the great cities of Europe or Asia are promising destinations. Others yearn for an African safari. One may be a winter sports enthusiast and would prefer to ski. The other may prefer deep-sea diving.

BETTIEQUETTE:

Reserve a longer, more energetic holiday for phase two of your honeymoon.

Consider two honeymoons. If you have different preferences, the answer may be to shorten the time on the post-wedding honeymoon and then, in a few months, plan a second honeymoon so both preferences can be accommodated.

Escape to a beach. A beach is ideal for a quick honeymoon because it's a good bet that after the months of planning your wedding, you're exhausted. Get away for at least a few days in a relaxing, pampering atmosphere.

Think about what you want from your beach holiday. Do you dream of the Caribbean, Bermuda, Hawaii, Fiji or the French/Italian Riviera?

Do you want an all-inclusive resort? A private villa? A small boutique resort? What experiences do you most want your beach honeymoon to deliver? Check out what various locations offer. If you do your homework, you may discover a host of options that had not occurred to you. You'll likely love being pampered with a his-and-hers massage. Perhaps you imagine a private patio with the sea just outside your door. Romantic dinners, interesting cuisine, a variety of sports, fascinating places to explore, rafting, deep-sea diving, snorkeling, great golf courses—anything goes.

Do the research. The planning begins with collecting pamphlets and articles and doing some Internet research so you can review all the possibilities. Stay in touch with a reliable travel agent who can keep an eye out for specials on your behalf.

BETTIEQUETTE:
You may want to go someplace for your honeymoon that your friends haven't yet discovered. Great for bragging rights!

Consider European beaches. The lure of the French and Italian Riviera is undeniable. And it delivers a memorable experience, combining sun and sea with lovely places to explore. The best-rated beach/sea honeymoon destinations in Europe include Santorini, Crete, Sicily and Cannes.

Price-shop to score a deal and the trip of a lifetime. Compare prices. Booking well ahead of time could save you a bundle, or you could come across a special.

Make a to-do list.
- Check that your passport is current.
- Find out what your destination's local currency is.
- Ask about what credit cards are most acceptable.
- Make copies of your passport and travel documents. When you're sightseeing, carry one copy on an inside pocket or, better still, a money belt. Do not carry them in your handbag. Leave one set in the hotel safe.
- Leave a detailed itinerary with family or a friend.
- Check health notices that relate to your destination.
- Take along your health insurance information.
- Make a note of your doctor's name and phone number.
- Determine if your destination requires immunization or needs vaccination certificates.

- Pack light. Experienced travelers take few clothes and can travel around the world with a carry-on. Make fashion choices that can do double duty, such as a swimsuit cover-up that works well as an evening top.
- Have everything important in your handbag or carry-on in case your luggage is lost: travel and hotel confirmations, makeup, medications, change of underwear, one change of clothing, money and credit cards.
- Leave your expensive jewelry at home. Your hotel room may not be secure and you don't want to invite unwanted interest on the street.

Choose seats and check flight time before you get to the airport. Choose your seats ahead of time, and check with the airline on the day of your flight to ensure it's leaving on time. You'll be exhausted after the wedding, and the last thing you want is to be miserable during the flight.

Check to see if your flight offers snacks. If the airline isn't providing free snacks, be sure to pack some. Choose nutritious, filling foods, like nuts, fruit and crackers.

Make your checked bag easily identifiable. Do something to make your luggage easily identifiable in the event that you need more than a carry-on. Tie a big, brightly colored ribbon on the handle, for example.

Lay off in-flight drinks. Avoid alcoholic beverages when flying. They are dehydrating, so drink lots of water instead.

Pack moisturizer in your handbag. Your skin will cry out for moisture during the flight. Keep lotion handy and use it hourly.

Dress for the destination weather. The plane sets down and you step out into glorious, hot weather. You're ready for fun, but take it easy. Strong sunlight and extremely hot temperatures can be dangerous when you're not accustomed to them. Dress for the weather: wear loose-fitting, light-colored clothing made from breathable fabric.

Limit your sun exposure. It's wise to limit your time in the sun, especially during the first few days. If possible, stay out of direct sun between 11 a.m. and 4 p.m., and always wear a hat, as well as sunglasses and sunscreen.

Sightsee with care. Wear a money belt if you're going sightseeing. It's the best way to safeguard your money, your credit cards and your emergency information. Carry hand sanitizers to protect yourself against questionable things you may touch.

Plan your honeymoon transportation well in advance. Whether you're traveling immediately after your wedding or a day or two later and if your destination includes flying, have a friend drive you to the airport or take a taxi.

Find out how you will get to your resort when you land. What is provided by the resort? Your package may include being met at the airport when you land. If not, inquire about airport taxi service and costs. Rely on your experienced travel agent about using taxis and leasing cars at your destination.

Get a flat rate for taxis. If a taxi does not have a meter, establish the price you'll pay before you get in and before the driver starts driving.

Do research on car rentals. If you plan to rent a car throughout your holiday, get rates in advance. Ask your hotel or, better still, your travel agent how to get the best rates. You can get stung if you try to negotiate uninformed at your destination.

Have a wonderful time, take plenty of pictures, and bring back beautiful memories that will last your whole life.

Honeymoon Roundup

Plan your honeymoon together.

~

Consider two trips to accommodate the interests of both of you.

~

Protect your valuables.

~

Pack light, choosing dual-purpose fashion.

~

Arrange your transportation before your arrival.

Test yourself.
Test each other.
I dare you.

Nineteen

Quiz Time

Check your relationship IQ

Answer the questions separately and then compare your responses. Check more than one answer where applicable. The answers will be revealing and sometimes surprising.

The goal is to start a conversation. So let's kick open the door to some honest communication.

Intimacy and Lifestyle

Marriage can change everything, including how to share your expectations with your partner.

Q: Will you have nights out with same-sex friends after you're married?

❑ Absolutely. We both need to maintain our friendships with our friends.

❑ No. I think we should see our same-sex friends as couples. Singles nights can get out of hand.

❑ Occasionally is okay, but weekly get-togethers with old pals is just hanging onto the past.

Q: Will you maintain your friendship with opposite-sex friends?

❑ No. It's too dangerous and invites the sharing of spousal problems that should be kept between the couple.

❑ Yes, but we should see these friends as a couple.

❑ Sure. Why not? We're all adults here.

Q: Will frequency of sex be maintained after marriage?

❑ Of course. Why not? We're getting married—not retiring!

❑ An initial passion when a relationship is new can't be maintained. It is replaced with a deeper love.

❑ Perhaps. But we need to be open about our individual needs and never use sex as a reward or punishment.

Q: Is it okay to keep secrets from each other?

❑ Yes. Details about my personal investments, loans and earnings are my personal business.

❑ Yes. We can protect details from our past, such as past relationships or bad debts. However, we do need to share everything current.

❑ No! We're not single people who happen to be living together. We're married and need to share everything.

Q: Would you care if your partner were to gain weight?

❑ I would have a problem with it because I take delight in my partner's good looks.

❑ I would be concerned because it could indicate that something in our relationship was in trouble.

❑ I don't care as long as the gain doesn't affect my partner's health.

Q: Who will control the TV remote?

❑ Compromise! One of us likes sports and the other likes sitcoms. We'll have to negotiate so we can stay in the same room!

❑ We will have two TVs—one in the family room and one in the bedroom. A little separateness is okay. To each his own!

Q: When you fight, who will you confide in?

    ❑ Everyone needs a confidant and most likely it would be a parent.

    ❑ My best friend is discreet and knows how to listen.

    ❑ Nobody.

It's not easy to share feelings or a past that we have put behind us. Total sharing may not be possible, but it can help your relationship if you are able to express what matters most to you with the person closest to you.

Neat Freak or Clutterbug

Are you compulsively neat or compulsively untidy? That includes an untidy mind! Get ready to examine your habits and discuss.

Q: My comfort level is with the following:

    ❑ Everything is filed away and out of sight.

    ❑ Everything should be within reach so I can access it at any time.

Q: When I shop, I . . .

    ❑ take a specific list.

    ❑ shop with an open mind.

Q: I keep appointments by . . .

    ❑ noting them on a piece of paper.

    ❑ recording everything on my computer or smartphone.

Q: I like my week . . .

    ❑ planned in advance so I can organize my time and anticipate each event.

    ❑ relatively open so I can change course on a dime because I like spontaneity.

Q: My clothes closet is . . .

❑ organized, with jackets, pants and shirts grouped.

❑ catch as catch can. My clothes do find a hanger. Occasionally.

Q: My car . . .

❑ is neat and tidy with no clutter.

❑ sometimes has leftover wrappers, papers and the occasional soda can.

Q: My socks/pantyhose are . . .

❑ neatly rolled and stored according to color.

❑ in a drawer and matched as I need them.

Q: I keep things I no longer need . . .

❑ out of sentiment.

❑ out of habit.

❑ I don't keep things I don't need.

If your responses aren't a good match, there could be rough sledding ahead. Don't assume that a neat person is the ideal partner. Some are compulsively neat. They may have more fun if they were a little more relaxed about their surroundings. On the other hand, a clutterbug has lazy habits, often assuming that the neat freak will pick up after them. (Check out if the clutterbug's mother took on that caretaker role!)

Sharing Space

Whether you will be living together for the first time or you're already living together, take time to test and compare your personal lifestyles.

Q: When I get home from work I like to . . .

❑ sit with a drink and relax.

❑ get dinner underway.

❑ watch TV.

❑ relax with computer games.

Q: Excluding sex, when I go to bed I prefer to . . .

❑ read.

❑ watch TV.

❑ settle to sleep.

Q: My job involves . . .

❑ bringing work home.

❑ leaving my work at the office.

❑ bringing work home and needing absolute quiet.

Q: Sharing housework . . .

❑ includes cooking and meal planning.

❑ has an exception. I don't cook.

❑ includes all home cleaning.

❑ doesn't work: women are better at household work than men.

❑ is better if we hire someone to clean.

Q: Sharing yardwork means that . . .

❑ we share cutting and trimming the lawn.

❑ we share taking out the trash.

❑ inside and outside, there are trade-offs.

Q: Our entertaining style means . . .

❑ being relaxed; sitting on the floor eating pizza.

❑ having a BYOB party.

❑ putting BYOB parties behind us.

❑ sitting at a nicely set dining room table.

❑ preparing a gourmet meal.

Q: I prefer seeing friends . . .

❑ in our home.

❑ in a restaurant, splitting the bill.

Q: At-home entertaining should be . . .

❑ once a week.

❑ twice a month.

❑ monthly.

Talk about your personal boundaries and expectations. As always, the details need to be resolved if you are going to live together without constant irritation. It all starts with communication—and a sense of humor.

Straight Talk about Money

Money problems tear apart relationships more often than any other problem. Confront and resolve any issues before your wedding day.

Q: How do you feel about a premarital agreement?

❑ Never. It's a bad start, indicating lack of trust.

❑ Yes. We have to acknowledge that 50% of marriages end in divorce.

❑ Yes. It avoids misunderstanding about who owns what.

Q: Let's talk about the cost of your wedding.

❑ I really want it to be over-the-top wonderful and don't mind taking on debt.

❑ I want the wedding we can afford without going into debt.

❑ I'm hoping our parents will chip in so we can have a great wedding.

Q: Have you given any thought to what age you would hope to retire?

❑ Yes. I have put money into a retirement savings plan since I started earning.

❑ You've got to be kidding. That's a street I won't cross for years.

Q: What means of saving works for you?

❑ I like to have a specific amount automatically removed from my paycheck.

❑ I tune in at tax time and sometimes borrow so I can get the tax benefit of a government plan.

❑ It's too soon to talk about saving. We're young. These are the years to enjoy life.

Q: What percentage of your family income should be set aside to cover an emergency?

❑ I try to put 10% aside. Some goes into saving for a house, some into a retirement plan.

❑ I invest in mutual funds. You have to start investing when you're young to protect yourself.

❑ I like shorter-term goals like saving for a house. Anyway, owning a house is probably the best return on investment over the years.

❑ I have no idea. What do the experts say?

Q: Under what conditions would you spend your savings?

❑ I consider it untouchable except for a calamitous health problem or unemployment.

❑ Life is to be lived, not spent squirreling money away. If having a major holiday meant withdrawing money, that's okay with me.

Q: To whom have you talked about getting professional financial advice?

❑ My bank manager has been very helpful in setting up a good program.

❑ I don't go to professionals. They all have their own axe to grind and their own product to sell. Their advice is biased, so I compare investments with friends.

❑ I read the business section of newspapers and watch investment shows on TV. I'm educating myself.

❑ No one.

Q: Assuming you plan to have children, will money be a factor in terms of deciding when the time is right to start a family?

❑ Absolutely! It is THE factor.

❑ Being ready to have a kid is an emotional decision. My great-grandparents were poor but managed to raise nine kids.

Q: Who will handle the money?

❑ She will. She is more organized and better about budgeting.

❑ He will. He likes to be in control, from spending, savings to investments.

❑ We will each handle our own money but both will contribute to a joint account to handle household expenses.

If you have been living together, you may already have resolved many of these issues. But play the game anyway. You may uncover a few surprises.

If you have had separate homes before marriage, you may get a wake-up call. It's the small differences that sometimes annoy and irritate you.

Planning Your Wedding

Will you have fun and deal calmly with mistakes, will you obsess over every detail or will you put yourself in the hands of a professional planner? This questionnaire is for the bride-to-be to clarify her own expectations.

Q: Are you a daydreamer about your wedding?

❏ No. My priorities are my friends and my job.

❏ Yes. I have daydreamed about my wedding since I was a little girl.

❏ Yes and no: I will make time to make it a special day.

Q: If possible, would you take a business leave-of-absence to concentrate on the wedding?

❏ You're kidding. Right? I'd be so bored.

❏ What a trip! I'd love to have a month to plan this once-in-a-lifetime event.

❏ Not a month, but a few no-guilt hours off here and there would be nice.

Q: Do you expect your parents to be involved in the cost of the wedding?

❏ No. We will host our own wedding. Our parents will be our guests.

❏ Yes. My parents have always assumed they would pay for my wedding.

❏ No. We will pay, but on the invitation will put our parents as hosts.

❏ Our parents have offered to share the costs with us.

Q: Do you both share in the decisions that relate to the planning?

❏ Not really. A wedding is really the bride's vision.

❏ Yes. He loves it all. Especially the registry!

❏ He has ideas but I'm the one who makes it happen.

Q: Do you have a vision about your gown?

❏ No. I will try on gowns with an open mind.

❏ Yes. I know exactly what best suits my body type.

❏ Yes and no. I will bring my best friend who has a great fashion sense.

Q: Your wedding cake options are . . .

❑ No wedding cake. Too expensive and the dessert comes with the meal plan.

❑ Yes. A cake is a must. It's part of the wedding tradition.

Q: Who will "give you away"?

❑ No one. I will walk down the aisle alone and be met by my fiancé.

❑ My father. It would break his heart if he didn't escort me.

❑ Both my parents. I want to honor my mother, too.

Q: How will you handle an intrusive mother-in-law?

❑ I have asked my fiancé to keep his mother at arm's length.

❑ I will include her in areas that won't interfere with my overall vision.

❑ I am being inclusive because she will be in my life forever. It's good insurance!

Q: How will you keep your boss happy?

❑ I don't even go online for wedding information at work. I keep it low-key.

❑ My boss is enjoying my excitement and is decent about the long lunch hours.

❑ I have to keep on top of the wedding planning at the office because there's so much to do.

Q: How will you satisfy divorced parents who don't get along?

❑ I won't be involved. They can't make their problems my problem.

❑ I'm sensitive to their concerns and will try to satisfy both.

❑ I will turn to a third person so I'm not required to take sides.

The bridal couple share the planning responsibilities—but they should accept help from family and friends. A professional wedding planner can relieve you of almost all the time-consuming effort, but you're on your own with relationship problems.

Your Love Affair

This isn't a quiz. We're just sharing information about how and where we meet our partners. Check out your experience against a Roper Center survey of one thousand men and women.

Q: Do you believe in love at first sight?
- ❏ Yes.
- ❏ No.

(Ninety percent of adults believe in true love. The male and female response was equal. Marital status and age made no difference.)

Q: Did you meet your partner online?
- ❏ Yes.
- ❏ No.

(Twelve percent met online, then in person, finally resulting in marriage.)

Q: Did you meet your partner through friends, family or at work?
- ❏ Yes.
- ❏ No.

(More engaged couples still meet through work, friends or family.)

Q: If you met online, how long should you wait before meeting in person?
- ❏ Same day.
- ❏ Next day.
- ❏ A week.
- ❏ A month or more.

(Seventy-five percent of singles say one to three days is reasonable. Men suggested a slightly earlier meeting than did women.)

Q: After the first meeting, did you recall whether a fragrance was worn?
 ❑ Yes.
 ❑ No.
(Seventy-three percent said they could recall a fragrance. The olfactory sense is more important than most realize.)

Q: How was the second date arranged?
 ❑ Phone
 ❑ Email
 ❑ Text message
 ❑ End of first date
(Both men and women preferred contact by phone, but 49% of men used text messaging and 29% used email.)

Q: Which compliment would mean the most to you?
 ❑ "You have a terrific sense of humor."
 ❑ "You have a terrific smile."
(Seventy-five percent of women chose "You have a terrific smile." Eighty-eight percent of men chose "You have a terrific sense of humor.")

Q: Who said "I love you" first?
 ❑ She did.
 ❑ He did.
(Men not only usually say it first, but they are twice as likely as women to say it in the first week!)

It doesn't matter whether you experienced love at first sight or have a relationship that began with friendship. All that matters is that the person you're planning to marry is the love of your life.

In the thirty-five years I have been responding to bridal queries, the questions—and answers—have radically changed because traditions have evolved.

Twenty

Ask Bettie

Answers to the Most Asked Wedding Questions

There are two primary reasons for the change in questions received from bridal couples. Today, the bride's father is rarely the sole person paying the piper. And today, the bridal couple is much older than couples marrying three or four decades ago.

The average couple saying "I do" today are working, have established careers, are often living together and are able and willing to host their own wedding—and have it their way.

So here's a taste of today's major quandaries. Maybe one or two will hit home with you.

Unwelcome Small-Fry

Dear Bettie: I am invited to a formal wedding to which children are not invited. I am breastfeeding, however, and feel that it is only fair that an exception be made for me. Do you agree?

I do not agree. A small baby can be even more disruptive than an older child. If you cannot express your milk and leave the baby for a few hours with someone you trust, this is a wedding you should not attend.

Gate Crashers

Dear Bettie: At my cousin's wedding, a relative brought along uninvited friends. My aunt had to beg the caterer for extra dinners and crowd tables to find seating for them. How should this have been handled to avoid this unpleasantness?

No one should cater to people who are gauche enough to crash a reception. To avoid a family confrontation, it can be turned over to the manager of the dining room. Regardless of who delivers the message, the explanation is that because they were not expected, they cannot be accommodated as there is neither food nor seating available. To keep the peace, they could be invited to come back later for the dancing.

Mom Plays Gotcha!

Dear Bettie: I dearly love Rob's parents, who are kind and loving, but they are not very sophisticated or knowledgeable about etiquette. My mother is a stickler. The parents have not met and my mother has dug in her heels and refused to initiate a meeting with them until she and Dad are invited to their home for dinner. Should I have Rob give his parents a nudge and tell them about their social obligation? I hesitate because this may embarrass them.

Your mother is playing gotcha and shame on her. Etiquette is about making people feel comfortable, not following rules. Traditionally, the parents of the groom invited the bride's parents to dinner, lunch or afternoon tea, but many of the old traditions are biting the dust. There are reasons: These days, couples are older when they marry and many are living together before marriage. Couples in their mid- to late twenties are much more in charge of the decision-making, which was once Mom's domain.

Don't stand on ceremony. Host a dinner yourselves to introduce your respective parents to each other.

Head-table Behavior

Dear Bettie: We recently attended a wedding where, as soon as everybody was seated for the dinner, the men took off their jackets, the women took off their shoes and they hooted and hollered throughout the meal and the toasts. My fiancé thought it was fun. I thought it was appalling. Your thoughts?

A wedding is not a college prom. Jackets and shoes stay on at the table. Freshening makeup is done in the powder room, not at the table. No smoking at a head table. Attention should be accorded those at the microphone. A wedding is a grownup event that calls for grownup behavior. Later, when the formal event translates into a party (and the older folks have drifted away) it can get down and dirty.

Groom's Choice

Dear Bettie: My fiancé would like to honor his father by inviting him to be his best man. I think this is unsuitable and putting a damper on some of the events, such as the stag.

It is not at all unusual for a son to have his father as his best man. Nor is it unusual for a father, at a second wedding, to have his son as his best man. Regardless, the decision is not yours to make; it belongs solely to your fiancé.

Dad Doesn't Pay

Dear Bettie: My aunt lives about 200 miles (322 kilometers) away and assumes that my father will pay for hotel accommodation for her and her adult children. My father is angry and says he will pay only if it is required by wedding etiquette. (My aunt always has been a penny-pincher and has Dad unnecessarily picking up bills all the time.)

Out-of-town guests are responsible for their own travel and accommodations. It is useful to get prices from local inns (and perhaps negotiate special prices) and enclose them with invitations going to out-of-town guests. When they receive this information, your aunt and her adult children will get the message.

Traditional Versus Trendy

Dear Bettie: Mom and I are at war. She's traditional and I'm trendy. I want to streak my hair in a rainbow of colors just to be very different from other, boring brides. I'm betting you agree with my mother, but I said I'd write to you.

It's your day, but here's an interesting test. Go to the library and look at books with wedding pictures that date back ten, fifteen, twenty years and decide which have stood the test of time. Then decide what look you want to have ten, fifteen, twenty years from now. The wedding is for the day. The pictures are forever. However, bottom line is that it's your choice.

Knotty Question

Dear Bettie: I attended a wedding where the ring was knotted so tightly to the little ring bearer's pillow, it took forever to get it loose. Everybody broke up! Must it be tied so tightly or, for the short trip down the aisle, can it be loosely tied?

Why not have drugstore rings on the pillow and pantomime retrieving them from the pillow—with the real rings entrusted to the best man and best woman?

Greed Run Rampant

Dear Bettie: My fiancé and I have spent a ton of money on other people's weddings and we want to reap the benefits. After the wedding service we will have a cocktail party—no dinner—with a cash bar. My mother is embarrassed, but it's not her money. Are you up-to-date enough to recognize that this is now acceptable?

Unacceptable. You should not host the biggest event of your life, spend all the money on yourself (gown, cake and much more), expect friends to give you wedding and shower gifts, and then ask them to underwrite the reception. Cash bars at a wedding are never acceptable. Greedy. Greedy. Greedy.

Female "Best Man"

Dear Bettie: My fiancé's oldest and closest friend is a woman and he wants her to be his "best man." I think this is inappropriate and would be happy, instead, to include her as a bridesmaid. Do you agree?

I don't agree. It is not uncommon for either sex to have an opposite-gender honor attendant. I attended a wedding where the three honor attendants of the bride were her three brothers. Your fiancé's best friend should be beside him. She should not be a bridesmaid because your honor attendants should be your own best friends.

Thanks, Friends

Dear Bettie: I am ordering embossed thank-you notes and don't know if, before the wedding, they should be from both of us or from me.

The notes should just have the embossed words thank you. The message must be handwritten. Say thanks on behalf of both of you for shower and wedding gifts before the wedding. Specifically mention what the gift is and how much you both will enjoy it. After the wedding, write your thanks as a couple. And see that the groom writes his fair share of notes.

Tongue-in-Cheek Invitations

Dear Bettie: We are thinking of having funny wedding invitations with our baby pictures on a postcard with the message "Who would have thought it?" My mother is having a fit but I think our friends will love it. What do you think?

If you're having a casual wedding, your friends will love it and also get the message that it's an informal get-together. If you're having a more traditional wedding, your invitation is sending the wrong message.

Anxious Singles

Dear Bettie: I think that having single women line up to catch the bride's bouquet looks like an act of desperation, suggesting that all single women are husband hunting. How do you feel about it?

I agree with you. Bouquet-throwing is gradually disappearing as one of those customs that has outlived its significance. (Similar to putting wedding cake under your pillow and hoping to dream of the man you will marry.) We can do without these customs. A nice option is for the bride to present her bouquet to her mother, or to have the bouquet made in two sections to include both mothers, or to keep it and have it dried.

Messy Cake Feeding

Dear Bettie: I hate, hate, hate the custom of the couple feeding each other wedding cake. It inevitably ends up with them game-playing and smushing cake into each other's face. Is this custom so entrenched that it is expected?

I hate, hate, hate it too! And for the same reasons. It too often becomes aggressive and embarrassing. But my response is personal and not based on etiquette. So if it suits the participants, go for it. If it doesn't, take a pass on it.

Who's Coming?

Dear Bettie: I have seen "number of persons attending" added to response cards. Does this help us and the caterer clarify the exact number?

Not a good idea. Inevitably some people will think that this is an invitation to add extended family. Some singles will add an escort that you did not intend to invite. Other guests may feel free to add their children. The invitation only extends to those whose names appear on the envelope. You would be opening Pandora's box. The guest list must always be well controlled.

Directing Traffic

Dear Bettie: I know exactly what I want in a bachelorette party hosted by my attendants: a dinner in a charming inn that is just out of town, a buffet dinner and everyone staying overnight so we really can party. Can I instruct my attendants?

If you want to arrange your own bachelorette party, you must host it and pay for it yourself, otherwise you'd be spending your friends' money without giving them the option of setting their own budget and making their own decisions. Similarly, shower decisions rest with those who are hosting the shower.

Teacher's Pets

Dear Bettie: I would like my class of about thirty students to come to the church to see me married but, of course, they would not be invited to the reception. I plan to have different invitations printed for them. How should this be worded?

Anyone who receives a printed invitation should be invited to the reception. Invite the class orally and give them a handwritten note reminding them of date, time and place. Exclude any formal invitation wording.

This gives me a chance to address an ugly pattern that has emerged recently in which some friends are invited to a wedding and reception and others are invited to join the party after the dinner. "A" friends and "B" friends. How insulting!

Where's the Gift?

Dear Bettie: My father threw a lovely party to announce my engagement, and my attendants gave me a huge shower to which some people were invited but did not accept the invitation. At the engagement party, some people did not bring a gift, and many of those who did not come to the shower also did not send a gift. Isn't that a poor show?

An engagement party does not require a gift, and a person who does not accept an invitation to any event is not required to send a gift.

Those close to the bride may not be able to attend because of a prior commitment and may decide to send a gift, but it should not be expected.

Reluctant Sister

Dear Bettie: My sister will be eight months pregnant when I am married and feels that she should not be part of the wedding party. I would be upset if she were not my matron of honor. Do you agree that she should be allowed to bow out?

My opinion doesn't matter. The only opinions that count are yours and hers. She needs to be specific about her feelings. Is she bowing out because she thinks her expanded size will be inappropriate in the processional and the photographs? In that case, she may just need reassurance. On the other hand, she may feel self-conscious and that being in the spotlight would spoil her day. Let her know how important it is to you, but allow her to make her own decision.

Thoughtful Gestures

Dear Bettie: A few guests are coming from a great distance and I so appreciate it. What extras can I do to acknowledge their extra effort and expense?

Good for you. Here are some thoughts:

- *Put a gift basket in their room at the hotel with homemade cookies, a bottle of wine, cheese, crackers and chocolates.*
- *If they haven't rented a car, have a local guest drive them to the service and the reception. Invite them to the rehearsal dinner (but not to the rehearsal).*
- *Have the MC acknowledge them at the reception.*

Consultant's Dilemma

Dear Bettie: I am a professional wedding consultant with a problem. I am getting married and, with running my business, I am feeling overwhelmed. Nevertheless, I feel that I should be able to do it all myself, and what is worse, so does everybody else. Help!

Delegate, delegate, delegate. You know all the reliable suppliers, so you can be the decision-maker, but ask your friends to step up to the plate to make it happen. Ask one to arrange for transportation for the entire wedding party on the day of the wedding. Ask another to help with table centers or guest favors. Ask another to help address and stamp envelopes. Spread the joy or you're going to be exhausted on your wedding day.

Spoilt Child

Dear Bettie: My sister is very insistent that her three-year-old be a flower girl at my wedding. Small children often are disruptive and they also upstage the bride. I've seen it happen. Amy is spoiled, loud, insistent on getting her own way. I see a family feud erupting and don't know how to handle it. Mom wants her grandchild in the wedding party, too, so I'm outnumbered.

It would be better if she were not part of the wedding party. If this is going to result in hard feelings, however, you can set ground rules.

- *If she is not ready to walk down the aisle, there will be no coaxing. She immediately will be whisked away to sit with her parents.*
- *If she makes it to the altar, she immediately will be seated with her parents.*
- *If there is any crying or shouting, she immediately will be removed from the service.*

Adamant Mom

Dear Bettie: My mother is very chic and has a strong personal style. She won't wear a corsage. I don't know why this upsets me, but it does. I really want the mothers and grandmothers to wear corsages so they look special. Who is right?

What your mother wears or doesn't wear is her call. As it is important to you, however, she may agree to carry a tiny bouquet, which would be charming. Some women prefer to clip flowers to their handbag. But don't push it.

Smoker Alert

Dear Bettie: I feel so strongly about smoking. I want it totally prohibited at my wedding and reception. My father doesn't agree— in fact he strongly doesn't agree! He says this is inhospitable at a large social event. Who is right?

You may think that a four- or five-hour social event without a cigarette is tolerable for most smokers, but it's not. They will leave long before the end of the reception. Ban smoking at the table (no ashtrays there) and in all areas where guests will be gathering. Have a separate smoking area, however, where they can escape periodically. You could have a small notice on the table that directs them to the area or have servers direct them.

Honeymoon Conflict

Dear Bettie: I am a skier and am never happier than when I am on the slopes, but my fiancé loves beach holidays where he spends most of his time snorkeling. So, you've guessed it, we have quite different ideas about the ideal honeymoon. Who wins?

You'll soon find out that marriage is about compromise. How about planning a very short honeymoon to one location and, a few months later, have a longer honeymoon at the second location—so everybody wins.

Stand-in Father

Dear Bettie: I do not have a warm relationship with my father and he is showing little interest in my wedding as well as not offering to pick up any bills. Should I have my fiancé's father walk me down the aisle?

Clearly you want to publicly punish your father. It can backfire, however, because humiliating your father will be what everybody talks about on your wedding day. Walk down the aisle on your own and have your fiancé walk toward you, joining you at the halfway mark, and approach the altar as a couple.

Few Guests for Groom

Dear Bettie: My fiancé's family lives at the other side of the country so only a handful of his family will be here for the wedding. I know that guests should be seated on the side of the church that represents the family, but his side will appear empty, so can we ignore this rule?

Rules of etiquette and tradition are misunderstood. They are only in place to simplify and clarify social situations. In this instance it is indeed more appropriate to fill in both sides of the church without regard to family connections.

Burnt Toast

Dear Bettie: We have been to so many weddings where the toasts have been embarrassing or too long or even vulgar and totally lacking in taste. I think too many people think they are Stephen Colbert. Tell us how to avoid this.

It begins by choosing the right people. If the best man, for example, is unreliable and lacking in discretion, you already know this when he is invited to be the best man, so you can expect to be on pins and needles at the reception. Set some ground rules to all who are giving toasts—advise them what is off-limits, how long the toasts should be, and to be mindful of the variety of listeners in terms of age and sensitivities.

Who Obeys Whom

Dear Bettie: Why do the words *obey* and *man and wife* still exist in some marriage vows? My girlfriend was blindsided at her wedding when, with no prior discussion, the priest used both phrases.

You must discuss this with the clergy conducting the service so there is agreement about the terminology. These days, many services do say "husband and wife" and omit "obey," but this is an issue that needs to be discussed prior to the service so there are no surprises. Also make sure the clergy does not intend to add a short but perhaps unwanted sermon.

Two Left Feet

Dear Bettie: We can't dance and we're both losing sleep over having all eyes on us during that dreadful first dance. Can we skip this tradition?

Sure you can. You may find guests holding back on going to the dance floor, however, because they are waiting for the first dance, so be proactive. You can have the MC invite everyone to dance. Alternatively, go onto the dance floor, take two steps, stop and invite your parents to join you. (This also eliminates the father–daughter dance and the bride's mother and groom dance.) Take another couple of steps, stop and invite your attendants to join you—and then everyone else. Alert attendants and parents ahead of time so they will cooperate.

Honeymoon Woes

Dear Bettie: My fiancé loves surprises. I don't. He wants to plan the honeymoon, tell me what climate to pack for and surprise me. I won't know the destination until we board the plane. I hate not being part of the decision of where I will go on my own honeymoon, have told him this, and it has resulted in an ongoing argument. But he's not giving in. He says I'm being a poor sport and this will add to the fun of our trip. Incidentally, these surprises have happened before and I feel shut out of the decision-making. What would you do?

This is about control and I hope you see the warning signs. This is not about pleasing you, when you have so clearly expressed your preference. It is about his controlling the major decisions in his life—and yours. I urge you to review your history with him. How many "surprises" has he insisted on in the past? The answer to your question is not what I would do, but what you will do.

Flower Budget Breakers

Dear Bettie: I am thunderstruck about the cost of flowers. Can you suggest ways to stretch the dollars but still have enough posies to be effective?

The cost of flowers usually is about 10 percent of the total wedding cost. This comes as a surprise to many couples, but there are practical ways to reduce the cost. Use fewer blooms in the bouquets and more "fill." Think about the most expensive element, table centers, and consider options other than flowers. If you want to cluster candles, get the approval of the site. Some do not allow pillar candles but may allow candles set in glass receptacles. Don't forget to delegate someone to remove the flowers from the service site and bring them to the reception where they can do double duty.

Double Wedding

Dear Bettie: Mom wants her and Dad to renew their vows at my wedding, her wearing an evening gown and coming down the aisle just before me and joining Dad and my fiancé at the altar. I have been shedding a few tears in the privacy of my bedroom. They are paying for the wedding, so am I being selfish and ungrateful?

Your mother obviously loves the spotlight and shame on her for not allowing you to have your own day. Have your father or a close friend of your mother point out that she is raining on your parade. She and your father should have their own ceremony on another day. Be firm about this. The fact that they are picking up the tab for your wedding has no bearing.

Just Cash, Please

Dear Bettie: Friends are asking me where I plan to register. The point is, I don't want to register because we want money. When I tell people this, they sometimes raise an eyebrow and shrug their shoulders, as if I don't have the right to express my preference. What gives?

A person giving a gift makes the decision about what they want to give. The idea of a registry is to give them some options on what you need or want. Many people prefer not to give money, so I urge you to register or, I promise you, you will get many gifts that you neither need nor want.

Hey! I'm the Bride and I'm the Boss

Dear Bettie: The two sets of parents are paying for the entire wedding and we appreciate that. Nevertheless, they seem to forget that I'm thirty-two years old and know exactly what I want—from how many guests (I think they're budgeting for too few), to the menu (they're cutting back on the seafood bar I want during the cocktail hour) to the band I want. As I said to my parents, "Whose wedding is it, anyway?"

My short answer would be, "Who's paying the bills, anyway?" If you want it your way, you should be hosting your own wedding. The person paying the bills makes the decision on size of wedding, expensive extras added to the basic menu and other extravagances. Perhaps you and your fiancé can quietly pony up for the extras, while the parents still host the basic wedding.

Small Wedding Options

Dear Bettie: We're having a small wedding—just fifty people. Are there things we can do to make it special and memorable even though it's tiny compared to most of today's weddings? Everybody who is really important to us will be there and five are actually coming from Germany, so to us it's a big deal!

Of course it's a big deal, and size has nothing to do with how memorable and special a wedding can be. In fact, you can add thoughtful details that would be impossible with a large wedding. If, in your invitations, you plan to offer a choice of entrée, you might have pretty menus at each place and personalize them. Have the name of each individual at the top of the menu, along with a short sentence about why they are important to you, and then their personal menu. As well, each person or couple could be individually welcomed in the toasts and their connection to the families or the couple explained.

Boycotting the Wedding

Dear Bettie: My mother has threatened to not come to the wedding if Dad brings his girlfriend—and my dad won't come without her. It's a standoff and, although I love them both, I'm disappointed in their dumping this in my lap and asking me to choose between them.

Shame on them. You have every right to be disappointed in them. Don't allow them to force you to decide between them. Your father's girlfriend could join him after the service, at the reception. Then plan for your parents to host separate tables at the reception. After you make this suggestion, tell them that both will be invited and what they do is between them, but you will not be put in the position of choosing between them.

Gifts for Attendants

Dear Bettie: I have four questions: Should all attendants receive the same gift? If not, should the same amount of money be spent on each? Is it appropriate to pay for their going to a hair salon on the wedding day in lieu of gifts? If this is okay, would you then give actual gifts to the male attendants?

Attendants do not need to receive the same gifts, but you should spend the same on each maid and a little more on your best woman (because more is expected of her during the wedding planning). You might choose a gift that would appeal to each, such as a gift certificate for a spa for a woman who loves spas or a piece of sporting equipment for the sporty attendant. A trip to a hair salon for your wedding is, truthfully, a gift to you, not to them!

Remember that this should be a joyful time in your life.

Twenty-One

How to Avoid the Ten Most Common Mistakes

1. Create a budget. Too many couples start making decisions before they set a budget and before they have a meeting with all those who will be involved in paying for the wedding. And they often don't understand that those paying the bills make the money decisions.

A wedding can be wonderful, whether it is big or small. Size is never an indicator of a wedding's success. Too many families splurge on an event that is too large and too expensive, resulting in debt, or, in the case of parents, dipping into funds that would be better invested in their retirement.

2. Don't choose a gown by committee. The fun and challenge of shopping for the bridal gown should not be shared with a group of friends. This is not a choice to be made by committee.

The bride should shop alone or with one person whose taste she trusts. (And, as an aside, the bride should beware of being too dictatorial about the bridesmaids' dresses if they are paying for their own gowns.)

3. Keep romance on the front burner. Too many brides get so involved with the wedding, they forget *why* they're getting married. So don't put romance on the back burner. Get away to a B&B for an occasional weekend and promise each other not to talk about the wedding. Avoid getting consumed by the wedding and make sure the emphasis is where it should be: on your shared future and goals. In the months before the wedding, keep romance and love front and center instead of allowing stress, indecision and decision-making to get in the way of your relationship.

4. Avoid etiquette misdemeanors. Wedding etiquette is just an extension of day-to-day etiquette, most of it based on common sense and being tuned in to others' feelings. The mothers-of-the-bride and -groom, for example, don't host showers because they are likely hosts of the wedding and double-dipping for gifts is considered excessive (even though we all know that, behind the scenes, the mothers are likely baking and helping out!).

Similarly, a bride shouldn't have input into what kind of shower she would like. A shower is a gift to her—so the how, where, when and who is up to the hosts.

Remember the following:

- People should not toast themselves.
- Gifts require handwritten thank-you notes.
- Bridal couples should not ask for cash as wedding gifts.
- The nature of a gift is always decided by the person doing the giving.

5. Get everything in writing. Every detail should be spelled out in a contract. Too many couples make changes or additional requests by phone instead of in writing (and without inquiring about the additional cost). Costs should be nailed down with every change so there are no surprises.

A final call should be made to all suppliers a few days before the wedding to confirm dates, locations and details. Be aware that nothing is the fault of the supplier if it's not in writing.

6. Keep the invitation list under control. Set the number of guests in stone. If you're inviting singles without dates, don't make any exceptions. If it's an adult-only event, don't be bullied by the person who won't come unless they can come *en famille*. And the hosts should not tack on last-minute names either. If one set of parents keeps adding names, it upsets the balance of the original, agreed-upon list. You will pay in hard feelings as well as dollars.

7. Don't become a diva or a groomzilla. It happens to the nicest men and women! They become so involved in their wedding, they begin to assume that the rest of the world is making it their life centerpiece as well. They forget that their family, friends and co-workers (even their boss) have full lives of their own and that, for them, someone else's wedding is just a pleasant social diversion.

Don't let the quality of your work suffer, spending work hours on the phone and computer or taking long lunch hours to plan your wedding so that co-workers have to pick up the slack.

Don't ask too much of your attendants. Stay tuned in to their personal lives and continue to have friends-nights-out that are not all about you and your wedding.

8. Pay attention to your health. Stress inevitably accompanies the pre-wedding months. This is, after all, the biggest event you ever will give, and yet it's just an add-on to your regular day-to-day life. There never has been, nor ever will be, a time when you will experience so much emotional pressure.

Regular exercise is important, but this is not a time for a quick-loss diet. If you want to lose or gain weight, the process should be slow and long-term.

If you wish to be your personal best on your wedding, your beauty and health plan should begin at least six months before the big day.

9. Shop carefully. Money has a habit of slipping away during the wedding planning period. Both bride and groom may purchase items that are not needed, resort to impulse buying and spend in excess of their budget.

And a caution about gown shopping: gown designers tell us that their names frequently are used illegally by people selling gowns online. Too many brides order from the Web and end up with a style or even size substitution. A wedding gown is a bride's most important purchase and too important to leave to chance.

10. Don't second-guess your decisions. Here is a mantra I wish were repeated by every bridal couple and all wedding hosts: *"Let it go!"*

The greatest stress arises when hosts continue to look at alternative ideas after they have made their original choices. When you choose the invitation, consider it done. Stop looking at all the things you *might have done*. Stop comparing other venues, other cakes, other menus after the decisions have been made. When it's done, it's done.

This should be a joyful time in your life. Don't let the planning overwhelm you. Take a deep breath, make your decisions one at a time, and once you have, don't keep looking over your shoulder wondering if there might have been a better choice.

So all together now:

Let it go!

Acknowledgements

There are a group of people who must be thanked, because without their being just a little pushy, my thirty-five years in writing about weddings may never have been collected in one place. They made this book inevitable. It started with Don Swinburne, publisher of *Today's Bride*, who reminded me of my extraordinarily long history of observing weddings and suggested I put my experiences on paper. James Young at Penguin Random House offered to pass a first draft on to others who might make it happen. Huge thanks to Penguin Random House vice president and Appetite publisher Robert McCullough, who encouraged my somewhat free-and-easy style because it made him smile. Scott Richardson, Creative Director, caught the spirit of the book and made it better than I could have imagined. And a hug to Penguin Random House editor Bhavna Chauhan, who gently challenged me. Whenever I said, "It's done," Bhavna would say, "I'd love to hear what you have to say about . . ." and there would be yet another chapter. As it turned out, it wasn't finished until Bhavna said it was finished!